BRILLIANT LEADERSHIP

www.amplifypublishinggroup.com

Brilliant Leadership: Patterns for Creating High-Impact Teams

This book expresses the author's personal views and opinions, not necessarily those of the influential company she works for. The author has written authentically and done her best to avoid errors, inaccuracies, omissions, or any other inconsistencies.

For more information, please contact:
Amplify Publishing, an imprint of Amplify Publishing Group
620 Herndon Parkway, Suite 220
Herndon, VA 20170
info@amplifypublishing.com

Library of Congress Control Number: 2024903878

CPSIA Code: PRV0324A

ISBN-13: 979-8-89138-134-6

Printed in the United States

This book is for all those who want to shine a little brighter.

Dedicated to my brilliant kids.
Shine on!

SUZANNE MARTIN

BRILLIANT LEADERSHIP

PATTERNS FOR CREATING HIGH-IMPACT TEAMS

TABLE OF CONTENTS

INTRODUCTION

* * *

WHY CULTIVATE YOUR LEADERSHIP STYLE?

"Frankly, I'm exhausted."

I nodded reassuringly. "Tell me what's happening."

She continued. "Don't get me wrong, I love my team, but I just can't get them on my wavelength. I'm spending all my time correcting their work on top of my other responsibilities, and it's too much. If things keep going as they are, I'm going to burn out. You know me. I'm not afraid of hard work, but this is stretching me beyond my limits."

"What do you think the root of the problem is?" I asked.

"I was hoping you could tell me. Maybe…I'm just not speaking their language. Perhaps you could put on one of your training workshops and explain what I need them to do and how I need them to do it. Could you do that?"

"I could," I replied. "But I think there might be a better solution…"

That conversation took place many years ago with the marketing manager in Vietnam—an incredibly smart woman we'll call Maya. She was a super-high performer with a type A personality who worked longer hours than everyone else and took every training course. She was accustomed to excelling in every role she landed.

However, the wheels came off when she became a manager.

Maya went from being a fantastic individual contributor to being the leader of a team, a position she was unaccustomed to and for which her previous experiences had done little to prepare her.

Maybe you can relate to her dilemma. Or maybe your challenge as a leader is different. Perhaps you don't have the level of influence you would like over your team. You might have a perfectionist streak that prevents you from letting your team shine. Or, you may struggle to motivate and bring the best out of the people in your charge.

Your challenge could be that you find yourself acting in a leadership role that you've been taught is effective, but that doesn't sit comfortably with you. There are few things worse than spending every day acting in a way that is out of harmony with your true self. Deep down, you probably know you need to find a way to improve in your role, but the demands of your work seem to make it impossible to find time to take yet another training course or workshop that may or may not be any help in meeting your challenges.

If so, let's try something different.

My name is Suzanne Martin and I've worked in learning and development for almost 25 years. I'm currently the Director of Marketing Learning and Development at Google. As part of my role I've coached hundreds of very smart people and helped them become the type of leader they need to be to excel in their role.

What type of leader do you need to be? It's different for everyone. Despite popular opinion, there is no one style of leadership suitable for all circumstances and effective for every person. In practice, I find everyone already has internal abilities to be the type of leader that is right for them.

It's just a matter of finding your own unique skills.

That individual difference is where this book differs from most other books on management and leadership. I'm not going to teach you *how* to be a leader, because I believe you already have that innate ability. Instead, I'm going to give you the tools to look inward and understand what *kind* of leader you need to be to reflect your strengths and your personality.

I gave Maya the right tools. We never did arrange a workshop. Instead, I asked her a series of questions and set a series of challenges that put her on the path to understanding what she needed to do to grow into her new leadership role and set the tone for the people looking to her to guide them.

Since that day, Maya has gone on to be a valuable leader across Google, YouTube, and Netflix. She attributes her success to the confidence she built up through the leadership coaching we completed.

Maya isn't an isolated example. There are many others who have graduated from my workshops or coaching that have gone on to do amazing things, and will readily proclaim the work we did together was a turning point for them. They, of course, did the real hard work, but I helped them build a launchpad from which to do incredible things.

At Google we don't create anything without first gathering and analyzing the data. Without that research you don't know where you're starting from or where you need to go. In the same way, you can't set out to grow and develop as a person and a leader without first gathering and analyzing the data about yourself.

By asking yourself deep, searching questions that get to the heart of who you are, what you want to become, and what you believe to be truly important in your life, you will achieve your desired growth. You'll find the critical questions within these pages.

Each chapter in this book is followed by a series of short exercises based on what you've just read. I encourage you to complete these exercises *before* you continue to the next chapter. Not only will this help you absorb the key points, but it will allow you to replicate some of the steps that my students complete when they attend one of my workshops.

By the time you've completed the last exercise at the end of the final chapter, you'll have all the self-knowledge and understanding you need to be able to find your authentic self and recognize the type of leader you're destined to become.

I consider it a pleasure and a privilege to have helped so many people grow and blossom in their career. As we take this journey together, it is my dearest wish that you achieve the same level of success and find true joy in discovering the kind of leader you were always destined to become.

Let's get started.

CHAPTER 1

PATTERNS OF SELF

* * *

WHAT KIND OF LEADER DO YOU WANT TO BE?

I took out my deck of cards and spread them, face up, so Geoff could see them.

"Obviously, this isn't a regular deck of cards," I said. "Each card represents a value. What I'd like you to do is pull out some of the cards that resonate with you."

"Resonate how?" Geoff asked.

"Think about your team and what values are important to you in terms of how you lead them and the working environment you've created for them."

Without hesitation, Geoff reached into the deck and pulled out the card labeled "*fun*."

"This is definitely us," Geoff said. "Above all else, we're a fun team."

"Okay," I replied. "So what is it about the way you lead that makes it a fun team?"

"We have a games room. It's really important to me that everyone has a place where they can go and relax and blow off some steam."

"That's nice. How often is the games room used?"

Geoff thought for a moment. Then he thought for a bit longer. He kept thinking.

With Geoff's permission I surveyed his team to get feedback on his leadership style. But he was still surprised to learn that "fun" was the last word anyone would use to describe him or their collective working environment. A more appropriate value would be: *work ethic*. Geoff was an incredibly hard worker who started early, finished late, and was capable of long stretches of intense focus. And while he may not have said it directly, the tone he set for his team was an expectation that they would have a strong work ethic as well. No one would dream of using the games room when he was around because they would have felt judged for stepping away from their desk for even a moment. They felt as though by taking a break they were falling short of expectations.

Geoff's team wasn't being critical. They liked and respected him, but the idea that they were a "fun" team was, frankly, amusing to them.

This differing perspective phenomenon is surprisingly common. A manager may have internalized a concept of what a leader should be, or what they want to be, but it doesn't reflect their own core values—what we sometimes refer to as their "authentic self." There's a gap between how they imagine things to be and the culture they've actually created.

A leader can *say* their team is service-oriented, oblivious to the fact that they've never once arranged a community service project, offered the team paid time off to volunteer at a homeless shelter, or held a fundraiser for veterans.

This divergence problem is more than just a source of light amusement for team members. Over time, a gulf between a leader's stated values and the reality of the environment they've created can rankle. People love to follow leaders they believe in, who are genuine, and who live their truth. Simply put, trying to lead in a way that doesn't align with who you are is unsustainable. You can fake it for a while and offer motivational speeches and aphorisms, but if your actions don't align, the trust your team places in you will eventually crumble.

Eventually, you end up with a dysfunctional team with low productivity, low motivation, and high turnover.

YOUR STARTING POINT

Unbalanced leadership doesn't need to be an inevitability. It stems from not putting sufficient time and effort into self-work. It's the one area people have a tendency to scrimp on or even skip altogether, because it's usually the most uncomfortable place to play. Building up your team and the business is much easier because it takes less emotional effort and zero introspection.

But there's no getting away from self-work. Trying to be the leader you think you should be, or that you *think* your team will respond to is pointless if it doesn't grow out of your core values. So identifying those values and qualities and finding your authentic self is always the best starting point.

Frankly, if you don't look inward now, you'll still have to come back to it eventually. Self-work should never be viewed as an optional extra. So, even if you've been a leader for many years—or even decades—it's never too late to turn your attention inward.

PERMISSION TO GATHER DATA

One important area of my work is 360 degree feedback. This is a process in which I gather anonymous feedback about a person's strengths and weaknesses from their manager, peers, and direct reports. The subject also completes a survey about themselves, and this allows them to identify gaps between what they perceive to be their leadership style compared to the perception of others. This is a valuable exercise.

I got my certification for this skill from the Center for Creative Leadership (CCL) in North Carolina, an institution that is world-renowned for its leadership research and training. They've worked with people and businesses all over the world, including a full two-thirds of the Fortune 1000. It's kind of incredible when you think about it. Leadership is such an important part of the world of business that not only have countless books been written on the subject, but there is also an entire non-profit organization with centers all over the world dedicated to answering the single question: how do you become a better leader?

The results speak for themselves. There are few, if any, who come away from studying with the CCL without a strong sense that they are in a better position to manage their team(s). And the research the CCL has completed confirms what you could probably have guessed—that leaders who develop their skills get higher performances from the people they manage and see a marked improvement in retention rates.

If you're reading this book, you probably already understand that developing your skills as a leader is not a luxury, or something you do to simply add a line to your résumé. Becoming a better leader is an essential part of your journey as a manager, whether you care for a small team of just a few people, or an organization of thousands. And if you weren't already convinced, then I hope you're starting to appreciate just how transformative these pages are going to be in your journey to become the kind of leader you want to be.

Your path to better leadership starts with gathering data.

In my work for both Pfizer and Google (but especially Google), companies always treat data with a healthy reverence. Gathering data is crucial if you're going to make business decisions that have the best chance of success. Developing your skills as a leader is no different. You can't adjust your mindset and your actions without first understanding who you are as a leader right now, and what type of leader you should become based on your internal values and personality. There is no one-size-fits-all in this area. It's unlikely that the CCL would exist if there were only one type of acceptable style of leadership and it was simply a case of following an approved template. But there are, in fact, an almost infinite number of styles of leadership that can all be dazzlingly effective when they match up with the right personality type embodied by a person who has learned how to leverage those abilities in the most effective manner.

Finding the right leadership style for you is an intensely personal journey and it's impossible to complete without giving yourself permission to look inward and gather data about yourself. It's only by completing this data-gathering exercise that you can start to create a roadmap that will lead to your own, individualized destination of becoming the leader that you want to be.

BEING A LEADER IS GROSS

My workshop on becoming a leader provokes all sorts of interesting reactions, but perhaps the most memorable response came from Deborah. I had barely finished my introduction before she exclaimed:

"Oh, gross! I'm not a leader."

I have to be honest; this is not the usual reaction I get from people attending a workshop on how to be a competent leader. But she grabbed my curiosity.

"Why don't you think you're a leader?" I asked.

"I'm a manager of a team of grown-ups. That's all. I'm not a leader. I don't walk around thinking I'm better than everyone else."

"Maybe there's a different definition of a 'leader' that would make you more comfortable," I countered.

"I doubt it. What an arrogant thing, to label yourself as a 'Leader.' The only thing worse would be to attend a class to learn how to be that arrogant."

It turned out that Deborah had been put forward to attend this workshop by her manager. And while she was initially flattered that he considered her to have the potential to become a leader, when it actually came to attending the class she had an almost visceral response to it.

I convinced her to approach the lesson with an open mind. Her mood started to change once we began talking about the idea of managers being seen as leaders by their team, and consequently having a sizable impact on the culture of the workplace. Because your team is looking to you to lead, your actions—or even inactions—will have an impact on the working environment. Deborah, despite having some pretty big hang-ups about the concept of being a leader, was in that role whether she liked it or not. Once she began to realize her team viewed her as a de facto leader, and that her focus and what she chose to talk about and address with her team shaped the culture, she had an epiphany.

Deborah realized that, whether or not she was comfortable with being a leader, that is what she was. People looked to her for guidance. How she responded to challenges, failures, and successes set the tone for everyone in her charge. She still had misgivings about the word "leader," but by the end of the session she was in a much better place in terms of being able to recognize the role she was playing and how much weight her actions carried.

Like Deborah, people often envision a leader as being a "great" person who knows all the answers and can resolve any issue with a stroke of genius. In some cases that may be true. But most of the time it's simply an individual who is in service to other people and is able to help someone get to the place they're trying to reach. That can happen whether you're in the leadership role because you've been assigned that position of authority, or simply when you find yourself in a situation where you're able to step up, bring a group together, set the tone, and inspire positive action.

One of my favorite leadership quotes (roughly based on a Gandhi quote*) is "be the change you wish to see in the world." If you're in a leadership role and you take little or no action, life is just going to happen to you. Meanwhile, your lack of impact on the people around you is, in itself, a significant impact. Just existing in that role is going to affect things, so you may as well get proactive and work to shape the way in which you interact with those around you.

Being a manager doesn't, on its own, make you a leader. Neither does attending a workshop on how to be a leader. Leadership happens when you decide to serve those in your team and take responsibility for what's happening. You have a choice. Are you going to be a manager who simply manages and pretends that this is all that's required of you? Or are you going to take up the challenge and lead by your words and actions?

ALL SHAPES AND SIZES

When Eileen began her career, her manager told her that she wasn't cut out to be a leader. He said she was too nice, too kind, and too willing to listen to others' opinions.

"You don't have what it takes," he told her.

Guess what? Her manager was a jerk. He only knew one way of working—steamrolling over people—and he couldn't even

* https://quoteinvestigator.com/2017/10/23/be-change/

conceive of the notion that there might be more than one way to take the lead.

Fortunately, she ignored her boss and decided to do things her way. She continued to be kind and thoughtful to the people around her. She found her strength, not by slamming her fists on the table, but by being inclusive and bringing out the best in the people around her. She went on to become a country head for her company and now serves on boards for multiple companies.

Eileen found her success by being true to her authentic self. She proved that leadership comes in many, many different forms.

Eileen's story reminds me of the faulty premise that there is one style of leader. Every now and again I'll come across a blog post that promises to share "the 10 habits of successful leaders." These articles make me chuckle because they seem to promise that if you simply replicate those habits in your own life, becoming an amazing leader will soon be within your grasp.

But as Eileen demonstrated, successful leaders, metaphorically speaking, come in all different shapes and sizes, which means their habits are also going to be somewhat different. Imagine what would happen if you were to attempt to mimic the behaviors and practices of a leader that has a different personality than you and a completely different set of core values? What if Eileen had tried to lead like her manager? Clearly, it would have been a disaster.

If successful leaders have anything in common, it's that they're true to their authentic self. They're not trying to be something they're not, and they've avoided the trap of trying to cram themselves into an ill-fitting mold.

REFLECTIONS

Devin's manager was troubled by her introversion. He felt she needed to be more outgoing and dynamic if she was going to grow into a leadership role. When she came to my workshop she thought—as did her manager—that she was going to learn how to become an extrovert.

I have a penchant for videotaping portions of my workshop and then playing it back to my students so they can see how they come across when they're presenting or role-playing scenarios. As an introvert, being recorded was, naturally, one of Devin's nightmares. But, to her credit, she rose to the challenge.

When she watched it back, however, what jumped out to her was how awkward and forced she appeared. She didn't have a big, booming voice or a big bundle of charisma, and trying to pretend that she did made her look strained and unnatural. Imagine if she had spent the next few years trying to be something she wasn't. Picture the constant drain on her energy of trying to maintain a persona that was totally inauthentic.

Of course, the lesson is that Devin didn't need to learn to be an extrovert. She needed to learn how to become the kind of leader who naturally fit in with her quiet, gentle, thoughtful nature. Looking at herself from the outside helped her to realize this important truth.

Are you ready to do the same?

REFLECTION QUESTIONS: PATTERNS OF SELF

- What kind of leader do you want to be?
- What kind of leader would your team describe you as being?
- What kind of leader might you have been falsely assuming you *should* be?
- How do you feel about the idea of someone referring to you as a leader?
- Is your work personality the same as your "at home" personality and, if not, why?

CHAPTER 2

PATTERNS OF FEEDBACK

* * *

WHAT IS THE DATA TELLING YOU?

One of the most turbulent occasions in my workshops is the moment when a group receives their 360 feedback. If you're not familiar with the concept, it's an exercise in which the individual is anonymously rated on a variety of different skills and abilities by their managers, peers, and direct reports. The participants will typically also answer the same questions about themselves.

If you haven't personally experienced this process, imagine for a moment that you have and that you've just received a sealed envelope containing the results. Are you eager to tear the package open and dig into the results, or are you nervous and hesitant? Are you expecting to receive mostly positive or negative feedback? How confident are you in that prediction? How are you going to feel if the results are not what you're expecting?

These are the thoughts I can see etched on people's faces when one of my groups receives their 360 report. Needless to say, the result is a lot of anxiety and, frequently, a lot of tears.

The good news is that reaction is normal. For most of us, a big part of our ego is deeply tied into what people think of us. Even just the idea that people might think less of us than we imagine can be a source of great emotional trauma. On top of this, human beings have the great ability to laser in on a red spot in a sea of green. We could receive 100 glowing reviews from those around us, but all we'll see is the one negative point that will then color our entire view.

While I don't encourage people to ignore the outliers in their results, I do remind them to keep anomalies in perspective. You can't please everyone all of the time, and you certainly can't expect everyone to like you all of the time. It's rare for a 360 feedback to contain zero negatives. But the key is to look for patterns. If you see similar positive comments from a number of different people, you can take that to the bank. Equally, if you see similar negative comments from different people, this is a clear sign it is something you would do well to address.

In many cases, people's 360 feedback is as they expect it to be. If someone already has a good notion of their strengths and weaknesses, the feedback often reflects this and the report simply prompts that individual to lean into their strengths and note where they can improve.

But for some, the results come as a massive shock. Whether they're considerably worse than they expected or considerably better, the end result is still tumultuous.

Hannah, for instance, had some strong feedback in her report and, because of the language used, she was confident that she knew who it was that had made those particular comments. Her response, at least initially, was quite negative. She had a low opinion of this particular person already and the feedback merely served to make her defensive.

Then something interesting happened. As Hannah continued through the report, she came across criticisms from other people that made the same points about difficulties in her personality, but they were communicated in a different, more gentle manner. It was still hard for her to accept, but it had a profound effect. There's a world of difference between receiving criticism from someone who cares about you and has your best interests at heart versus someone who clashes with you. Hannah was able to lower her guard, think deeply about the feedback she'd received, and accept that she had room for improvement.

In this instance, Hannah, an ethnic minority, had worked hard over the years in building her confidence and having the courage to speak up and put her voice into the room. Her efforts had proved to be very effective in helping her progress in her career, but it seems she may have gone too far in the other direction. She was speaking so much in collaborative situations and was so insistent on getting her point of view across that she was drowning out the opinions of others in the room. As a leader, she was stifling some of the people around her.

For Hannah, progress in her abilities as a manager meant maintaining her assertive, confident posture, while also finding a way to do so that empowered the people around her to contribute and develop their own confidence.

Hannah's story illustrates what discovering patterns within

your leadership feedback can do for you.

Imagine nine out of ten people say you're an empathetic leader, and only one person says you're unfeeling. You should note the outlier, but you can be confident that you're doing well in this area. But if it's two or three people viewing you negatively in this area, then this begins to look like a pattern. It doesn't necessarily mean you are categorically lacking in empathy, but it definitely indicates that there is something in the way you are dealing with people around you—at least some of them—that is having a negative impact.

In one of my sessions, a gentleman was confused by his 360 report because opinion on him, in many areas, appeared to be split down the middle. This is a different kind of pattern, but it's still a pattern. Perhaps it means he was showing up for some people and not for others. Perhaps there is a difference in the way he deals with people in face-to-face meetings, compared to how he interacts with people through video conferencing.

A pattern, no matter how conflicting or uncomfortable, is an indication that you need to dig a bit and try to figure out what's going on. And once you understand what's happening in that space between you and the people you work with, you can make a decision on how to handle it. You may decide to consciously work on improving in that area or change your approach entirely.

You may even decide you don't want to change. Perhaps that critical feedback is just a manifestation of a cherished value system that you believe is working for you, and you prefer not to tinker with it. That's your choice, but the main thing is to be intentional in your decisions. If you're constantly bouncing around between trying to be what you think you should be, what you think other people want you to be, and what you actually want to be, you're going to come across as unsteady or even flaky.

Remember that this is all about figuring out the kind of leader you *want* to be. Feedback tools are invaluable, but they're there to provide you with information to help *you* make that informed decision, not to funnel you down a path you don't want to travel.

In this section I'm going to run through some of the most popular feedback tools available and help you figure out which are going to be most effective for you. This is not an exhaustive list, but it includes the tools and assessments in which I'm certified and that I've found to be most instructive during my last twenty-five years of coaching. I encourage you to choose and make use of one or two of them, but if you don't fancy investing time and energy into a formal process, I've provided a simple questionnaire that you can use to help you analyze your strengths and values at the end of the section.

JOHARI WINDOW
UNDERSTANDING YOURSELF AND YOUR RELATIONSHIPS WITH OTHERS

Overview

Joseph Luft and Harrington Ingham created this technique in 1955. The Johari Window is a communication model used to help people better understand themselves and their relationships with others.

The Johari Window is divided into four quadrants: open, blind, hidden, and unknown.

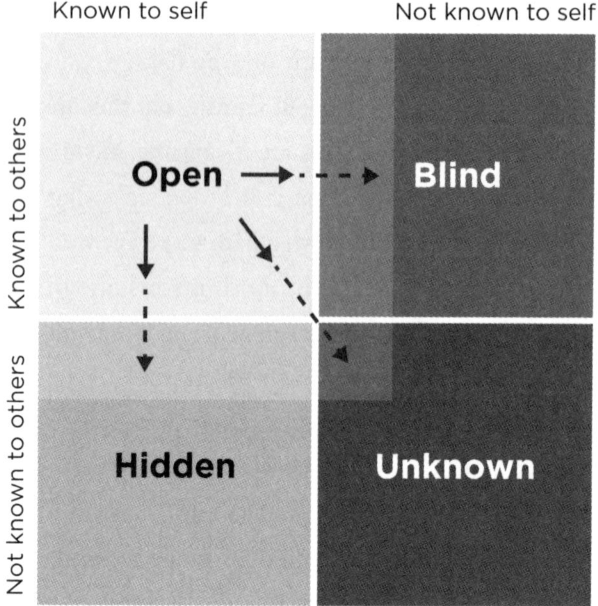

The **OPEN** quadrant is information that is known to both the individual and others. It includes things like your name, age, job, and hobbies. This information is usually easy to share and discuss.

The **BLIND** quadrant is information that is known to others but not to the individual. It includes things like your body language, tone of voice, and mannerisms. This information can be revealed through feedback from others.

The **HIDDEN** quadrant is information that is known to the individual but not to others. It includes things like your fears, dreams, and goals. This information is usually kept private because the individual feels it is not appropriate to share.

The **UNKNOWN** quadrant is information unknown to the individual or others. It includes things like your potential, talents, and abilities. This information can be revealed through self-discovery or feedback from others.

Purpose

By understanding the different quadrants of the Johari Window model, leaders can better understand themselves, build trust, improve communication, and develop new skills. For example:

- **Increase their self-awareness:** By understanding the different quadrants of the Johari Window, leaders can better understand themselves and their strengths and weaknesses. This can help them make better decisions and improve their leadership skills.
- **Build trust:** By sharing more information about themselves with others, leaders can build trust and rapport. This can help them create a more positive and productive work environment.
- **Improve communication:** By understanding how others perceive them, leaders can enhance their communication skills. This can help them avoid misunderstandings and build stronger relationships.
- **Develop new skills:** By exploring their potential, leaders can identify new skills they can study and practice. This can help them grow as leaders and contribute more to their organizations.

Use Case

Donna is a new manager in hardware. She's excited about her new role, but also nervous. She doesn't know her team very well, and she isn't sure how to build trust and rapport with them.

One day, Donna begins reading about the Johari Window. Intrigued by the idea that she can build trust and rapport with her team by sharing more information about herself, she decides to give it a try.

The next day, Donna begins by sharing some personal stories with her team. She tells them about her family, her hobbies, and her dreams. She also tells them about some of her challenges and struggles.

At first, Donna is nervous about sharing so much personal information. But she's surprised to find that her team is receptive and supportive. They start sharing their own stories with her, and stronger relationships begin to develop. Over time, Donna's team continues to be more open and honest with her. They are more likely to share their ideas and concerns with her. They also trust her more.

Donna's experience shows how leaders can grow by using the Johari Window. By sharing more information about themselves, leaders can build trust and rapport with others. This can help them create a more positive and productive work environment.

Pros

+ Simple to use
+ Free tools available online
+ Especially useful for leaders

Cons

– Can oversimplify the subject matter

INSIGHTS DISCOVERY
PERSONALITY PROFILE ASSESSMENT

Overview

Based on Jungian psychology, Insights Discovery (ID) is a psychometric tool created by the people development solution company,

Insights Group. The assessment takes the form of a quiz in which you have to choose words you believe do and don't describe you. Once completed, you receive a lengthy report containing insights about your personality, attitudes, and working style. The unique element of ID, and what makes it so memorable, is that it gives you insights into the type of energies you hold within. Broadly speaking, these are broken down into four colors.

- Fiery Red
- Sunshine Yellow
- Earth Green
- Cool Blue

The colors are placed onto a wheel and divided by two axes—the Thinking/Feeling scale and the Extrovert/Introvert scale. This information can provide valuable insights into the type of energy you naturally bring to a team and where your energy comes from.

For example, if my colleague, Jenny, and I are presenting a training and development event for an audience, we both bring high levels of energy, but the way in which our energies change and develop during that hour are substantially different. I'm an extrovert (red or yellow) so, when the workshop is finished, my energy levels are way up and I'll be wanting to go out to dinner with the group just so I can spend more time talking and engaging with them. Jenny, on the other hand, is an introvert (green or blue), so her preference is to go back to the office and take a little quiet time to reflect on the event. We're both refilling our stores of energy, but in very different ways.

It isn't quite as simple as grouping everyone into just one of four colors. It works on a scale so, in practice, some may identify very strongly with one area, whereas others may identify with two to a more modest degree. The above example demonstrates the former, but the latter is more common.

Purpose

A common misapprehension about ID—and in fact with most psychometrics—is to presume that it's a stereotyping tool that puts people into neat boxes so they can be properly handled.

There's no doubt that psychometrics *can* be used this way, but it certainly doesn't mean that they *should*. Just because one of your team members, Brad, identifies closely with the Fiery Red sector, doesn't mean Brad is only red. Further—and this is crucial—Brad isn't *only capable* of being red. He prefers red, sure, but he's perfectly able to step across into any of the other colors if the situation calls for it.

The real power of ID, and similar tools, is that they:

- Allow Brad to become aware of where his strengths lie and how he can adapt his behaviors to allow him to lean into his preference.
- Allow me, as his manager, to adapt how I work with him so that he's operating as much as possible in his comfort zone.

Another fantastic use of ID is to complete the assessment as a team and plot everyone's results onto a single color wheel. The results are always fascinating because it gives you an insight into the overall make-up of your group and the predominantly leaning direction of the team. This also allows you to observe color gaps in your team and know where this might be putting extra pressure on individuals. For example, if Earth Green is not well-represented on your team, there will still be times when certain members will be required to move into this color to get certain parts of their job done; it just won't be comfortable for them. This might reveal that you need to add some more diversity to your team to balance things better.

I also believe it's worth mentioning that ID, as with all of these tools, is only as useful as your willingness to study it and make relevant changes to your working and leadership practices. Otherwise it just becomes an interesting horoscope, for which you've paid quite a bit of money, that quickly gets buried under a stack of paperwork.

Use the tools, share the key highlights with others, and make practical plans to implement what you've learned. Typically, when my students complete an assessment of any kind, I encourage them to share the results with their teams (if they're a leader), their manager, and their peers. This encourages them to follow through and take action, but also helps those they work with to understand them better and improve their working relationship.

Pros

+ Reduces conflict in the workplace
+ Improves understanding of yourself and others
+ Can be completed as a team

Cons

- Beware of possible stereotyping

CLIFTON STRENGTHS*
DISCOVER AND BUILD ON YOUR STRENGTHS

Overview

Developed by Gallup, the global analytics organization, CliftonStrengths (CS) is a one-hour quiz that tasks you with repeatedly choosing between two different descriptors (or selecting the neutral option). The resulting report focuses on your individual strengths.

There's something about this tool that really warms me, focused as it is on getting people to lean into their strengths rather than agonizing over their weaknesses. It's an overwhelmingly powerful message and it can prompt really positive, encouraging conversations with your team members.

Purpose

Because the CS reports are not as in-depth as some other psychometrics, it's an excellent option when you're working with a large group and you don't have the ability to do group debriefs. When a psychometric test includes information about someone's weaknesses it can prompt a negative or anxious reaction from some and it's important to be available for them. CS avoids that issue because it focuses exclusively on strengths.

This is also the main weakness of CS. As much as I love the optimistic tone of this tool, I also believe it's important to know where you may be lacking in some areas so you can address them and avoid letting them become your Achilles' heel. Without that knowledge you can wind up with damaging blind spots.

* Formerly known as Clifton StrengthsFinder

A second, albeit minor, objection is that some of the codifiers are a little unusual. If, for instance, you're a lively person who likes to create a party atmosphere, CS describes that strength as being "Woo." Some people like the playfulness of the language, but I've definitely seen people reacting to the labels as if they find them condescending or just odd. Naturally, these non-typical descriptors can also make them difficult to translate into different languages or cultures.

With those reservations in mind, however, this is still an excellent, tried, and trusted tool. It's inexpensive, creates useful, encouraging results, and is one I often come back to.

When Would I Use This Tool?

It's a good choice when I'm working with a new group in which a foundation of trust has not yet been built. It's hard to go into conversations about weakness and blind spots with people you don't know well, so CS is a good place to start with teams that are still getting comfortable with each other.

Pros

+ Produces positive, motivational results
+ Inexpensive

Cons

- Doesn't address weaknesses
- Quirky terminology

HOGAN ASSESSMENT
PREDICT WORKPLACE PERFORMANCE

Overview

There is some crossover with the Hogan Assessment (HA) and Insights Discovery (ID) in that they are both personality assessments. The key difference is that whereas ID is primarily about an individual's personality traits and how they relate to others, HA is also focused on performance in the workplace, how they will likely fit into an existing team, and environments that could hinder their career development.

The output is weighty and comes in a beautiful binder, with multiple tabs to separate the information into different contexts. For instance, one of the tabs focuses on that person's connection with leadership, covering their strengths in this area, as well as potential challenges, and suggested motivators.

Hogan Assessments recommends that you have a certified HA practitioner run the assessment so they can provide personalized feedback on the results.

Purpose

Individuals can use HA to help develop their career, or even identify new opportunities that may better fit their strengths, weaknesses, and interests. Employers also use HA to assess potential hires and how effective they are likely to be in a particular role or operating within a particular team.

Use Case

Adam was struggling with his job in sales, primarily because he just didn't enjoy the role. As his coach I wanted to help him improve, but it was clear that he needed to find a new track. The problem was that he didn't really have any firm ideas on what he wanted to do, other than stop working in sales.

We used the HA and, sure enough, he scored very low in his suitability for sales work. However, it showed Adam could instead embrace his entrepreneurial leaning and preference for having space to manage his own projects. So he pivoted his career to focus on starting his own business where he could have more end-to-end control.

Pros

+ Useful for both employers and employees
+ In-depth reports are well-explained

Cons

- Can be expensive compared to other profile assessments

SCARF

RECOGNIZING YOUR TRIGGERS

Overview

Created by David Rock, author and founder of the Neuroleadership Institute, the SCARF model of assessment is designed to identify how people are differently affected, both negatively and positively, in social situations.

SCARF is an acronym for the five key areas that influence our behaviors:

- **Status** - relative importance to the people around you.
- **Certainty** - ability to predict what's going to happen.
- **Autonomy** - control over events and decisions.
- **Relatedness** - how safe we feel among others.
- **Fairness** - sense of fairness between people.

Purpose

Neurologically speaking, everyone is triggered by different things, in different ways, and to different extents. Because of these differences, it can be easy to upset someone without meaning to and without even realizing we've done so. Learning what our personal triggers are, and sharing them with those we work with, can help people be more empathetic with us. Equally, better understanding the feelings of others provides the opportunity to adjust the way we communicate or manage people on an individual basis and, thus, make their work life less stressful.

When Would I Use This Tool?

I use the SCARF tool both with teams and in one-to-one coaching sessions. The Neuroleadership Institute has a free, short assessment questionnaire you can use, but you can just as easily use the SCARF concept as the basis for a discussion and invite people to consider which of the five elements they consider to be their most sensitive trigger.

Pros

+ Improves interpersonal relationships
+ Free and easy to use

Cons

- Can be difficult to discuss triggers at work, especially with a new team

Starting with assessments is a good beginning and a way for people to begin to understand themselves and each other. Once you have a baseline and common language, you can start to go deeper into team dynamics.

ANOTHER PERSPECTIVE

One of my favorite things to do in my workshops is get out of the classroom, away from the lectures, and into some kind of real world experience. I often go on a field trip to The Rubin Museum of Art in Lower Manhattan, New York. If you've never had the pleasure, it's a series of exhibitions of Asian art, which is filled with the most beautiful paintings, sculptures, and drawings.

We begin by taking a guided tour, and then I break everyone up into smaller groups to wander around on their own. Once we've regrouped I invite people to share what they've discovered. Typically, during this debrief, someone will pick up on the fact the layout of this museum is quite different to other art exhibits. While other museums tend to focus on collections of works by individual artists, the Rubin Museum groups their works by dynasties or tribes. Interestingly, many of the works are also missing a personal signature, and instead have a collective or dynastic seal.

Our field trip, and the collective and dynastic seals in particular, brings home the fact that none of the work we've been doing in leadership, self-assessment, and looking for patterns in responses exists in a vacuum. Regardless of the industry in which we work, the type of work we do, or even the size of our organization, we're all part of a group effort. And that group is made up of many people with differing personalities, interests, strengths, and weaknesses. It's the kind of truism that is easily acknowledged and soon forgotten. But when I present it to people through the lens of a tangible, memorable experience—such as attending the Rubin Museum—it stays with them long after we've parted ways.

In the above example, we now have a good foundation for discussing those two different styles—artwork that is individually signed, and artwork that is presented as part of a group effort in which the individuals are not necessarily named. This is a beautiful analogy for team projects in which sometimes personal contributions need to be acknowledged and championed, and in which sometimes the group effort needs to be the focus. This discussion always takes us to some surprising places and no one forgets it in a hurry.

This is just one method for turning a field trip into a learning experience. When you're helping your team self-assess, consider finding a local museum or something similar and use it as a basis for creating a memorable lesson. You don't need to find a gallery as unique as the Rubin Museum. You can simply send your group around the exhibits and invite them afterwards to share what they think key pieces mean or represent. The differences in people's perspectives will come through strongly and will highlight just how different everyone's point of view can be, and how valuable it is to obtain and embrace diversity of thinking.

A consultant for the New York Police Department (NYPD) with whom I worked has her own spin on this method. She pairs people up and invites one person to describe a piece of art to their partner who has their back to the exhibit. The partner then has to draw, on a piece of paper, what the other person is seeing in the artwork and then share it to see how the interpretation has come across.

The value of looking at things through the lens of another cannot be overstated. Looking at people and the world from different angles helps to build up your empathy muscle which will serve you very well when you're leading team meetings or dealing with conflicts. Practical workshops that take you out of the office and into the real world are a fabulous tool for helping your teams understand the value of self-assessment—not just for understanding ourselves, but for understanding those around us.

NOTHING IS SET IN STONE

I've been fortunate enough that, because of my line of work, I've had reason and opportunity to become certified in many different feedback tools. In any given situation I have a whole range of options I can call on to assist the person or group in front of me. But what I've discovered is that you need to find the right tool for the right situation.

If you want to rely on a single tool that is going to become your primary aid for yourself and for your team members, this is perfectly valid as long as you're aware of the limitations of your choice. There's no feedback tool I'm aware of that works perfectly in every situation.

If, however, you want to give yourself more options and invest in a variety of tools, you need to become really familiar with the pros and cons of each so you don't wind up forcing the wrong feedback process on the wrong person. As a general rule of thumb,

I like to begin with the Johari Window (JW) and then, if more depth is required, move onto Myers-Briggs Type Indicator (MBTI) or the Hogan Assessment (HA).

JW is a great place to start because it's quick and easy to use and provides a really good foundation for getting the participants to open up and talk about their strengths, weaknesses, and working styles. It widens your aperture for yourself and then, in turn, for the people around you. As you work your way through the four quadrants, you'll be opening up an understanding of things that the individual knows but hasn't yet shared with others, the thing that others know but aren't known to the individual, and the things that neither parties know that are yet to be uncovered. It's simple, inexpensive, doesn't take up lots of time, and yet it provokes some fascinating conversations and insights. It's almost impossible not to come away from a one-on-one or group discussion, built around JW, without new and useful insights.

It's also a great introduction to the entire concept of using feedback tools and how to use them, not just as a curiosity, but as a means to understand yourself better and, therefore, help others to do the same. It's a great backdrop to potential future investigations and therefore is my preferred choice as a starting point.

If I decide to go deeper and take someone through MBTI, it isn't just about getting more insights, it's also about helping the person identify their preferences. This is really important to bear in mind, because once you start digging into more in-depth feedback tools, as well as gaining new information, you also potentially gain false negatives. There's been criticism over the years because MBTI, as well as similar tools, are based on Jungian psychology which, while still popular, isn't necessarily scientifically solid. But

I think whatever your point of view on Carl Jung, you can still pull a lot of value from tools if you simply acknowledge that the end results are only part of the story.

Survey assessment tools typically take the form of a series of word choices, and the participant is asked to choose or order their preferences. But because people's preferences, to a certain degree, can change from day to day, it is entirely possible to take the test twice and get different results. That doesn't make the test useless—the differences are usually minor—but it also doesn't mean you have to accept the results as gospel. If, for instance, the results say you're an extrovert and you don't feel that this is accurate, that's absolutely fine. You can choose which parts of the results you accept and which you don't because the real benefit is getting you to think deeply about these concepts, look inward, and understand yourself better.

Think of it like an artist painting a portrait. The end result is going to be affected by the artist's perception of who they *think* you are, and you may or may not feel like the picture is a true reflection of what you believe you look like. It will mostly be accurate, but if some parts of the painting aren't to your liking, you don't need to change yourself to suit the picture; you can simply accept the image for what it is: an interpretation of who you are.

You can choose to embrace some parts of the interpretation and reject other parts. The important thing is that *you* make that choice and then use that self-knowledge to decide what you're going to share with other people in terms of who you believe yourself to be.

That's how I encourage people to view the results of MBTI, HA, and others. Use these tools to gain some interesting insights, and then use those understandings to go even deeper. For instance, if there's an insight that doesn't sit right with you, it's an opportunity to ask yourself why you don't feel comfortable with it. Is it simply inaccurate, or is it because you have an innate need to be viewed in a certain way and the assessment conflicts with your desire? It's the "why" behind your reaction to the results that is most revealing and therefore most important.

Ultimately, if you don't like what the feedback is telling you, it's your choice whether or not to take it onboard or reject it. You have control. It's up to you, and you alone, how you want people to perceive you, and how you communicate and work with them as a result.

Interestingly, sometimes the personality type the tool reveals can, in itself, indicate whether or not someone is likely to be accepting of the results. When someone, for instance, requests to take the test again because the outcome is not quite to their liking, 99 percent of the time they tend to be people that fall into the "blue energy" quadrant. Why? Because people with this personality leaning are often perfectionists, which leads them to suspect that the discrepancies in their results must be a result of them making some "wrong" word selections. By contrast, I've never had anyone in the "yellow energy" quadrant ask to retake the test.

These provisos are also why I wouldn't rely on these tests to help me make hiring decisions. It's great for coaching sessions, and exploring someone's personality and working style, but using it for shallow candidate categorization would, in my view, not be helpful and could even be prejudicial.

IT'S NOT THE GOAL TO PIGEONHOLE

One of the common criticisms of feedback tools is the risk it brings of forcing people into a category and discouraging them from stepping outside of their comfort zone. This is a legitimate concern, but leaders can mitigate it by addressing any apprehension with the person or team, right from the start. But the onus is also on you, as a leader, not to use someone's feedback results as a way to pigeonhole that person and suppress their ability to develop new skills and modes of working.

Have the stereotyping conversation with whomever you're taking though these processes and make sure they're cognizant of the fact that their results are an opportunity to identify strengths and weakness, and subsequently grow. These tools are certainly not an excuse to shrug their shoulders and decide that some skills or promotion opportunities are beyond them. This activity is a starting point, and not a conclusion. No one should put themselves in a box and act as if they've just had their fate mapped out for them.

Also, no less important, be sure you don't yourself treat this person as if they are now a two-dimensional being about whom you know everything. If you walk away from a workshop saying, "Oh, okay, David on my team is 'blue,' so he's a detached extrovert and I should never ask him to deliver a presentation because he won't want to do it and will probably fail if he tries," you're making dangerous assumptions that can significantly impact his career—and your team. David's status as "blue" is a preference and not a cage. He might not be naturally enthusiastic about the idea of public speaking, but that doesn't mean he can't stretch himself into new areas and learn to become skilled and confident in them.

If you want to use your knowledge of David's preference for "blue" qualities in a positive way, think of it as a way to understand how to get the best out of him in any given situation. David can think quickly on his feet if he needs to, but because it's not his preference, it would be helpful to him and your team if you try to give him room to prepare and think through the situation before asking him to contribute to an important decision. That doesn't mean you can't trust him in a pinch because David can rise to the occasion and push himself out of his comfort zone if required, but he will no doubt be appreciative if these moments are the exception rather than the rule.

STRENGTHS BECOMING WEAKNESSES

If you've completed a Johari Window exercise with your team and want to do something more that isn't as in-depth as an MBTI or an HA, CliftonStrengths is a good next step. It's less intense and time-consuming, and also helps to maintain an optimistic outlook, without running the risk of getting into negative spaces around unexpected feedback results. That said, you can deepen the effect of this assessment by using the results to identify corresponding weaknesses and even consider how those strengths could themselves become weaknesses.

When someone identifies one of their strengths, you want them to feel empowered to lean into that ability and use it to improve their work performance as well as gaining insights into the direction their career can take that will make them feel the most confident and inspired. But if you jump to conclusions at that point, you miss a valuable opportunity to balance things out by finding the corresponding weaknesses. We don't want to dwell on our weaknesses—that can be discouraging—but we need to have an awareness of it so it doesn't become an Achilles heel for us.

For instance, if I want to be a CEO someday but I hate delivering presentations, that will almost certainly hold me back. So, I can either reject that ambition and say, "hey, that's just not who I am," or I can work on this skill, gain confidence, and turn that weakness into a strength. Or, at the very least, turn it into something that I can handle comfortably when it's required. It may never be my preference but it won't be an anchor holding me down.

And while my strength as a sociable, outgoing person is going to help me build loyal teams who enjoy working with me, that same positive quality could become a negative if I take it to the extreme and gain a reputation for sucking all of the oxygen out of the room. Or I could be a really motivational person who can, off the cuff, deliver a morale-boosting monologue, but become so enamored with my own voice that I lose my ability to listen to others.

Here's a really fun exercise: When your team has identified their strengths, invite them to take each in turn, imagine it magnified to the extreme, and see what negative effects it can produce. It doesn't have to be the case that they're already seeing those weaknesses, but the idea is to be aware of the potential for that to develop if they lean into their strengths but don't take the time to self-assess and recognize when they're pushing things too far.

As with pretty much all the exercises in this chapter, it's important that, whatever the results of the analyses, everyone is encouraged to write down their findings and the steps they intend to take as a result. Inevitably, some personality types won't care to do so, but they need to be encouraged to follow through, otherwise the benefits can soon be forgotten. One of my colleagues, Michael, is a great people person and an incredible connector. However, he hates writing business plans. He has such an aversion to it. Michael, I love you, but you have to write these things down. No doubt he would feel the same about writing out his thoughts after an assessment tool session.

Which neatly illustrates *his* strengths and weaknesses.

PROXIMITY BLINDNESS

We already discussed 360 degree feedback, so I won't labor the points. But I want to touch on it again briefly because if you are going to use this powerful tool, you need to be mindful of the different ways in which people will perceive their results.

Recall that most people see a healthy set of positive (green) comments when they review their results, but typically one of two things then happens. They either ignore the sea of green, and focus on the handful of negative (red) comments. Or they focus purely on the green and don't acknowledge the red at all. It's the difference between negative or positive personality types, and neither of those outcomes are desirable.

You need to help your team to see the full picture. That means appreciating the greens and using those elements to boost their confidence and reinforce their strengths, but also recognizing the reds as a gentle reminder that there is always room for improvement.

If someone gets a very mixed 360 result, or a sea of red, this can be more challenging to address. Depending on their mindset the individual can become very depressed or very defensive and dismissive of the whole exercise. You can help them work through this scenario by encouraging them to think about how much better off they are now, with this knowledge to guide them. Before, they didn't know they had blind spots, but now that they do, they're empowered to do something about it. And, hey, it's not like they were massively failing before. They were—and still are—successful in lots of different ways. Imagine how much better they'll be able to perform if they address these issues that have been brought to their attention and build on their existing foundation.

All in all, 360-degree feedback is simultaneously the most powerful and most challenging of all the assessment tools. If you decide to use it, make sure you're well-prepared to help the participants work through their feelings around the results and come up with a plan to use the information they've uncovered.

CULTURE MAPPING

Developed by author and professor Erin Meyer, the Country Mapping tool (often referred to as the Culture Map) allows you to select the country of origin of each member of your team, and create a chart that shows how differing cultures may affect a person's interactions in the workplace.

On the surface this sounds problematic because diversity and inclusion promotion has encouraged us not to "other" people. But this isn't about stereotyping or trying to put people into discrete boxes. It's about acknowledging that the culture in which we were raised had an impact on us, and that two people from different cultures, working together, will inevitably have to figure out how to harmonize their outlook, their working methods, and their communication styles.

For example, in some cultures, team members and team leaders will talk to each other as if they are friends. Whereas in any other cultures, deference to management is considered mandatory. In some cultures, people tend to learn better by studying in a classroom setting, other cultures lean more toward learning by watching and doing. Obviously, no one is a perfect reflection of their culture—there are other factors at play—but the impact is significant enough that being aware of the differences can be helpful in figuring out how best to work with, manage, and help people develop their career.

Where this gets interesting is when you directly compare two different cultures and observe the similarities and differences. People from Country A might have a similar communication style to people from Country B, but be at complete odds when it comes to leadership. People from Country C might have very similar approaches to leadership as people from Country A, but have completely different communication styles.

This likely isn't a tool you would use if the majority of your team are all from the same location. Creating a country map in which all but a couple of people are from the same place would probably only serve to make the minority feel isolated. You might want to privately use this tool to learn more about the people on your team who are outside of your cultural experience, but I wouldn't suggest carrying this out publicly. However, if you're part of a global organization, and your team members hail from several different parts of the world, this can be a good option—not just for your as their team leader, but so that individuals can learn more about their colleagues and understand some of the differences that need to be considered when collaborating.

You need to go into this kind of exercise with a lot of humility. This absolutely isn't about elevating any one culture above another, and if you as the team leader give off any signals in this area, this will backfire spectacularly. Use this tool as a learning experience for everyone involved and encourage an open-minded approach from everyone.

This also extends to the individual learning about their own culture and how it's impacted them, perhaps in ways they didn't appreciate before. This can result in some fascinating conversations in which individuals recognize some elements of their behavior that are products of cultural influences but don't actually represent their own authentic self. What starts out as an exercise to learn more about others can unexpectedly become an exercise to learn more about ourselves.

DON'T BLAME THE LETTUCE

One of my colleagues at Google, Kerri Jacobs, created a course called "Leading With Empathy." She begins the day by introducing the class to Thich Nhat Hanh, a Buddhist monk and teacher who created a beautiful word picture to describe how to view conflicts or breakdowns in relationships without resorting to blame or recriminations.

The concept is simple—if you plant lettuce in your garden and it doesn't grow, it would make no sense to blame the lettuce. In fact it probably wouldn't even occur to you to do so. Instead, you would get curious. Did it need more sunlight? Did it need watering more frequently? Did it need nutrients added to the soil? You'd figure it out and try again.

So, too, if one of your team members isn't performing or is behaving in a way you're not happy with, instead of blaming them, get curious about the "why." Look to yourself first and consider if there's something in the way you're leading them that is less than optimal. Next, have a conversation with that person and find out what they need to flourish.

Maybe I'm frustrated because Brad never responds to my WhatsApp messages. I ping him repeatedly and he only replies one time out of ten. It's frustrating and it's slowing things down. Am I going to just assume he's rude and incompetent? Or am I going to get curious and figure out what Brad's preferred style of communication is? Maybe he likes to keep his social media muted so he can be more productive. Maybe he prefers getting a phone call so he can give a quick response, there and then. Maybe he's feeling overwhelmed with work and he's struggling to keep up, and needs some extra assistance from a colleague.

This is a great attitude to adopt in work and in your personal life. Conflicts and disappointments are inevitable, but when they occur, rather than immediately looking to assign blame, look to yourself. And then get curious about what you can do to understand the other person better.

"When you plant lettuce, if it does not grow well, you don't blame the lettuce. You look for reasons it is not doing well. It may need fertilizer, or more water, or less sun. You never blame the lettuce. Yet if we have problems with our friends or family, we blame the other person. But if we know how to take care of them, they will grow well, like the lettuce. Blaming has no positive effect at all, nor does trying to persuade using reason and argument. That is my experience. No blame, no reasoning, no argument, just understanding. If you understand, and you show that you understand, you can love, and the situation will change."

*— Thich Nhat Hanh**

YOUR PERSONAL OS

We've covered a lot of tools in this section and this is a long way from being an exhaustive list, but whichever one you choose, make sure you utilize it fully. Don't be tempted to repeat the exercise multiple times a year, using different assessments. Doing so would be overwhelming for most of your team and dilute its effect. Repeating one type of assessment once per year and using it as an opportunity for everyone to take stock and think about how their lives and working habits have changed over the last twelve months is useful. But any more frequently than that and it becomes redundant.

Because, ultimately, these tools are only as effective as how you will turn the results into actionable steps. That's "you" as the leader of the team. Yes, it starts with you. Always.

Most high-performing leaders I know have a handful of personal

* https://www.goodreads.com/quotes/153586-when-you-plant-lettuce-if-it-does-not-grow-well

stories they can share at a moment's notice that instantly makes you feel like you know and connect with them on some level. If you don't already, you should build a small repertoire of your own. But as we already touched on, this only works if those stories align with your authentic self and the values you claim to uphold.

So, if you're telling people you're all about joy, and bringing joy to your customers, and joy to your colleagues, and joy to the department, when you stand up in front of your team to tell them your personal story it had better be about how important joy is in the way you connect with the world, and not about how you like to suffer for the sake of your career.

All these elements have to come together. It doesn't have to be today. Or even tomorrow. Identifying and embracing your core values, and developing your shareable stories so your team can understand who you are and what you stand for takes time to settle in your mind. But it needs to happen sooner rather than later.

A friend of mine uses a process similar to this and out of it has created his own unique operating system. His personal operating system, if you will. He has a sheet of paper that briefly describes his values, his working style, and how to get the best out of him, and he literally hands this to his team members and colleagues so they can short-cut the "getting to know each other" phase. This is, of course, even more effective if you *and* your team do this. Your Personal OS might include items such as:

- I'm a morning person, so please avoid asking me to do things after 6:00 p.m. On the flipside, if you need to reach someone who you're confident will be up at 6:30 a.m., I'm your gal.

- I'm an introvert and I prefer lots of thinking time. So if you need to discuss an important issue with me, please give me a heads-up so I can show up prepared.
- I only check my emails twice per day (beginning of the day, and end of the day), so if you need to reach me urgently, a phone call or an instant message is best.
- I'm not a naturally confident public speaker but I've worked hard to become one. Don't be afraid to ask me for help with a presentation or a public event.

This is a great conversation piece when you're onboarding a new team member. Tell them a little bit about your values, and how your team communicates, and then present them with your Personal OS (or, if you prefer, you can refer to it as a "cheat sheet"). Explain that this is to help them get the most out of your working relationship, and then encourage them to create one of their own.

And if they need a little help putting it together, that sounds like a good opportunity to book a session to help them use your preferred assessment tool and find their own patterns of feedback.

It's a shame that "data" has become a somewhat scary word. We connect it to things like security breaches, and profiling, and intrusive advertising. But really, data is quite benign. It's just information. It's what you do with it that makes it a force for good or a force for something else.

Always remember that part of it. Whether you're using assessment tools to look inward, or to help your team to do so, the end result is just data. It can't hurt you. It can't tell you what to do. And it doesn't change who you are.

It's just patterns in the noise—feedback on how we interact

with the world around us and the people in it. Learn from it, accept the parts that help, reject the parts that don't, and you will better connect with those around you.

KUDOS TO YOU . . .

I'm a big fan of old-school handwritten notes. Although now that I see that typed out, it makes me a little sad that handwritten notes are now considered to be something of the past. It's a heartbreaker because there's something about a personalized message that you can physically hold in your hand that transcends any amount of well wishes sent by email or instant message.

This is why I believe a greeting card is one of the best things you can send someone to congratulate them, commiserate with them, or thank them. It's the kind of thing people keep in a drawer and bring out whenever they need to be reminded that someone out there cares about them. Or, they forget about it and rediscover it years later and get to enjoy those good feels all over again.

Handwritten messages are the gift that can keep giving for years—potentially even decades.

At one of my workshops I set up a collection of little white boxes, each containing the name and photo of an attendee. Alongside the boxes was a big stack of little white cards and some pens. The idea is that whenever someone has a good interaction with another attendee during a break or a mealtime or a session, they can write them a little note and drop it into their box. They can decide whether to sign it or leave it anonymous.

It could be a great question, a helpful comment, an enjoyable chat, an appreciation for someone's friendly disposition, or anything, no matter how small, that someone enjoyed. There's a dual effect to this because, on the one hand, people get to receive lovely handwritten messages that they can enjoy and take away with them. On the other hand, everyone at the workshop gets to practice the art of being on the lookout for things they can commend.

The second benefit is a wonderful skill to learn. The only way to be alert enough to spot opportunities to commend people is to be completely present in the moment and to move your attention entirely away from yourself and focus it on what other people are saying and doing. As a leader, this is one of the greatest gifts you can give to your team, not just because it will make them feel good, but because it will also give them confidence, inspire loyalty, and help them to feel appreciated and content in their role.

What happens if nobody at the workshop gets a message in their box? As the workshop host, I'm also allowed to post messages to people, so I keep an eye on the boxes and I make sure everyone gets at least one message. Tricks of the trade!

REFLECTION QUESTIONS: PATTERNS OF FEEDBACK

- How did you respond to the last meaningful criticism you received?
- How well do you know your team members' personalities beyond their work abilities?
- Have you completed (or are you planning to complete) a feedback assessment?
- Has your team completed (or are you planning to complete) a feedback assessment?
- Are you familiar with your weaknesses and how you can turn them into strengths?
- Are you familiar with your strengths and how they could potentially become weaknesses?
- What have you done (or are planning to do) to assist and empower any members of your team who are, in some manner, a minority?
- When was the last time, if ever, that you blamed "the lettuce?"

CHAPTER 3

PATTERNS OF VALUES

* * *

ARE YOU IN THE DRIVER'S SEAT?

There's an old truism that children are far more likely to imitate what their parents do than what they say. And while your relationship as leader with those in your charge is not a parent/child paradigm, we all still have that instinct to imitate the behaviors of the people we spend the most time with.

This is especially true with the manager/employee relationship because you have a lot of power over the people in your team. You can help or hinder, promote or fire, praise or criticize, reward or punish. Your team's awareness of this will, to a greater or lesser degree, lead them to look to you for cues on how they should behave.

You may not be comfortable with this reality, but that doesn't mean it isn't true.

Your behavior and attitudes in the workplace affect the people you manage—no one is seriously arguing against that—but what many overlook is the extent to which this is happening. Your work practices and the way you talk to people, the things that you do unconsciously without even really thinking about it, can impact people in all sorts of significant ways, both for good and for ill.

Becoming aware of your behaviors and figuring out how they might be impacting those around you is a valuable exercise, and figuring out how your values tie into your style of leadership is key. This is why Patterns of Self (from chapter 1) is so important. You're the leader, so it starts with you. Understanding who you are and the values you hold will help you understand why you operate the way you do and, in turn, why your team responds to you in their particular ways.

By this point, hopefully, you've used some of the assessment tools to get a better understanding of who you are and what you care about. That self-knowledge is going to help you interrogate what you do and say in the workplace and recognize important truths. Not just whether these actions align with your values, but whether those values are inspiring your team to do their best work and find joy in their occupation.

Understanding your self-knowledge might be the hardest part of your entire journey. You know a lot more about yourself now and what you care about, and you can even articulate this to people coherently. But will this new found confidence and drive survive contact with the real world?

There's a whole other layer to this interplay between your values and your team's values, because it is inevitable that some people will bump up against your style of leadership. Not because your style of leadership is wrong, but because it doesn't align with their own perceptions of themselves and what *they* care about. You can do all the work to make sure your authentic self is perfectly aligned with how you present yourself, but that doesn't mean everyone is going to automatically connect with you on a deeper level. Many will, and it's more likely to happen if that congruence is there, but some people will still struggle with your approach.

This doesn't mean you're doing anything wrong—unless your authentic self is toxic. Differences are just an inevitable consequence of a workplace melting pot. But it can still be unsettling. It's even more bothersome if you do the hard work to line up your values and behaviors only to discover that team members who were once in sync with you are now struggling to fit in with some of the new leadership methods you're employing.

It's understandable if you become frustrated, feeling like you've fixed some problems only for others to emerge. The good news is that, even though this is the hard part, it's perfectly manageable with a little creativity and a lot of patience.

COMPANY CULTURE DOESN'T EXIST

A lot of people are attracted to come and work for Google because of the advertised work culture. Of course. Who wouldn't want to work in an office that boasts subsidized massage therapy, bowling alleys, free restaurant-quality food, and discounted haircuts? But I would argue that those things are not culture, they're job perks.

Yes, to a certain degree, a company-wide commitment to things like environmental sustainability and promoting a healthy work/life balance can leach through to individual departments, and provide a certain level of cultural considerations. But all of these things can be quickly drowned out by the more localized cultures which are created and evolved by human beings.

From this perspective, company culture, especially within large organizations, isn't real. The only thing that truly exists are individual human beings, and when you group some of them together into a team or department, an entirely unique culture will emerge.

As a leader, are you going to drive the culture or are you going to let it drive you? That's really a trick question, because in your position, you are going to set the tone whether you intend to or not. I've seen this happen on more than one occasion where someone comes in from another business, takes over leadership of a department, and simply expects the culture to match what the company portrays in the media. It never works out that way. *You* are in the driver's seat for the culture of your department, and while every individual will contribute to it in some way, these are small nudges on the steering wheel compared to the person who has their foot on the pedals.

If this is news to you, don't read on without taking time to really let this sink in. Think about it and write down some notes to yourself.

- I am the driver
- I set the culture
- People are looking to me to lead
- People will stay or leave based on my actions
- It has nothing to do with the company and everything to do with me

Embracing the knowledge that you, as leader, set the tone, can be a huge awakening. It has nothing to do with great coffee machines or nap rooms; leading has everything to do with how you comport yourself. This reality can be empowering, or it can be stressful (or both), but it's a reality nonetheless. And once you know, you can't unsee it. You'll start to have mini epiphanies around the simplest of actions because it will now occur to you to think about the potential impact of actions you previously took for granted.

For example, let's say you're an early riser and every Sunday morning you have a couple of hours to yourself before the rest of the family gets up and the chaos begins. You choose to use this time to get a head start on your Monday morning work and you often spend this window emailing your team about what's coming up over the next few days and what you'll need from them.

There's nothing wrong with this habit in itself. However, you now recognize that nothing you do in relation to your team is neutral, so you might wonder if this pattern is setting a culture that, in this department, we work on a Sunday. That isn't your intention. A healthy work/life balance is company credo and one of your personal values. You actually don't have any expectations that anyone will read your emails until tomorrow. You simply want it to be in their inbox, ready to go when the work week officially starts. But your actions might be sending an entirely different message.

What will the impact of that be? Maybe nothing. Maybe everything. Some of your team may be strict about ignoring work emails on a weekend and refuse to open it until Monday morning. Some of your team may feel resentful about their recreation and family time being interrupted on a weekend. Some of your team may feel pressured into also working on a weekend, and will respond to your emails the same day, giving up some of their free time to demonstrate their commitment to your lead. Some may be completely indifferent to whether or not you do a little bit of work early on a Sunday morning.

But whatever the effect, that's a lot of "maybes" you now have rattling around your brain.

What you choose to do about these thoughts, only you can answer. You could talk to a couple of senior team members and ask them for their thoughts. Maybe you start adding an addendum to your emails stating that you're just getting a head start on the week, and you don't expect (or even want) any responses or actions until Monday morning. Or perhaps you use the "schedule send" tool for Monday morning, or you could conclude that the impact is negligible and nothing needs to change.

Whatever you decide, the goal is to be intentional with your leadership and intentional with your teams. Don't do things on autopilot or because "this is the way we've always done it." Get curious about your work habits and routines, and think about your impact on the office culture. Discover and work on any conflicts between your stated values and the potential perceptions of your actions, even if those perceptions are misplaced. Continuously check in with your group about how they're thinking and feeling so you keep reinforcing your messaging and the culture you're seeking to build.

LIFE AND DEATH DECISIONS

Kathy Pearson, a mathematician and statistician at Wharton Business School, hosts one of my all-time favorite workshops. She includes an exercise in which the group is tasked with making a decision on whether a NASCAR race should go ahead. The attendees are given a series of facts, such as the weather, the ground conditions, the state of the cars, etc. After discussing, they have to agree whether to "red light" or "green light" the event.

Once the attendees make a decision, Kathy reveals that that data she provided wasn't for a NASCAR race at all, but was actually the exact script from the ill-fated launch of the Space Shuttle Challenger which tragically broke apart seventy-three seconds into the flight, resulting in the death of seven astronauts.

The result is typically a stunned silence as everyone mentally puts themselves in the NASA mission control center and how they would feel if they had been the one to make the decision. Naturally the mood of the exercise is vastly different depending on whether the group chose to "red light" or "green light" the launch.

The purpose of the exercise is to encourage the group to think about how they make their decisions, and recognize that there is a limit to how much you can rely on the data. Because, in this example, for all the detailed information provided about the launch conditions, the most important piece of data (that the rubber seals between two segments of one of the rocket boosters had been compromised by the cold weather) was missing.

That's the reality of data-driven decisions. You'll never have enough facts to make perfect choices. Data is valuable, but eventually you're going to have to make a decision and live with the consequences. Sometimes we try to put off making tricky decisions, hoping that someone else will decide or that the situation will resolve itself. But a leader needs the ability to recognize when they've done all they can to gather information, and that it's time to go one way or the other.

Fortunately, most of the decisions we make won't be life or death.

Communication is a good place to start because it's an area people often take for granted, and it's harder than ever these days given the huge volumes of text and video content everyone is consuming both in work and at home. Sometimes leaders, especially senior leaders, make this assumption that everyone knows what they think because they sent an email telling them about it. That's adorably naïve. Everyone might have received the email, and most of them might even have opened it, but how many of them read past the first paragraph before they lost interest or got distracted?

You can't rely solely on emails to communicate your critical messages.

As you progress in your career, and the size of your team grows, this is increasingly the case. If you have a team of 100 people, it becomes impossible to have one-to-one conversations with everyone, and then there's the temptation to frequently—maybe too frequently—email everyone, with the aforementioned problems. There is a way to encourage and train your teams to read your emails promptly and completely, so you can mitigate some of these challenges, but at the very least, your comms needs to be reinforced with other measures.

If you're leading very large teams, or groups of teams, much of your communication is going to be passed down through the descending hierarchies. It's easy to assume that everything you say is being communicated with precision down the chains, but that's rarely the case. Even if you're a master communicator that can elucidate your thoughts with precision, and know with great confidence that what you're sharing is being fully understood, that doesn't mean your message is going to be relayed with the same level of accuracy.

I see a lot of cascades start to crumble at the most senior levels because the message is being transmitted three to four times, like some kind of corporate telephone game. The leader cascades to the VPs, the VPs to the directors, the directors to the team leaders, and finally the team leaders to the team members. If even the gist of your original message has survived, you've done exceptionally well.

If you're in that position, think carefully about your comms process and how it can be reinforced at each level to keep things consistent. Especially if you're seeking to establish a particular culture, the precision of your communications as they move from level to level is paramount.

For leaders of a smaller organization this is less of an issue. But then you might, instead, want to think about the frequency of your touchpoints. Do you spend too much time out of the office, relying on others to fill the void in the cultural input? Or are you a "helicopter manager," excessively micro-managing everyone's work? Or are you spacing things out nicely, but making the process too one-sided and so not getting sufficient input from your team?

Of course, communication is just a start. There are a multitude of other areas within your responsibility where you may wish to spend some time reflecting, considering how your leadership style is impacting the overall culture. It's a complicated, messy business, but then people are also complicated and messy. A culture made up of flesh-and-blood humans is always going to be elaborate and knotty.

It's not everyone who gets to sit in the driver's seat and decide what the culture of the workplace is going to become. If you wear your values like a badge of honor and convey them in all of your interactions with your team, in time your shared culture will become a beautiful reflection of those standards. Enjoy the challenge. Embrace it.

CLASH OF THE VALUES

It's disappointing when you've done the hard work to uncover your values and put them front and center in your work life, only to find that they clash with the people around you. You may find that, after you've gone through this initial part of your journey, some of your managers, peers, or team members are simply not aligned with you anymore. Sometimes this misalignment happens because you've let go of or changed certain practices that only existed because of what you formerly believed you were supposed to do. Other times, these misalignments were always there, somewhat unnoticed, but now that you've fully crystalized your values it's become clear how large the gaps are.

When I see someone going through this experience I often see knee-jerk reactions. The realization of how far apart you might be from those you work with can be jarring, and it can be tempting to take drastic measures and seek to find a new position or even a new company.

In extreme cases that may be warranted, but most of the time this is an overreaction. Significant differences in values can be uncomfortable, especially when you first become aware of them, and can become blown out of proportion in your own mind. And yet, much of the time, the work needed to bridge those differences is far smaller than the gulf that separates you.

I also frequently see the other side of the coin in which someone recognizes that their values are completely misaligned with those around them and they decide to become a martyr. They commit to staying in the role, way past a normal time frame, unable to change the system around them, blaming everyone else for their predicament, and becoming increasingly frustrated and bitter.

A middle ground exists here and it starts with a little patience and a willingness to explore and understand other people's values with an open mind, rather than dismissing anything you instinctively don't like as "wrong." There's huge value in talking to people who have different mindsets and working styles and uncovering why they operate the way they do and what some of the benefits are. You might not like everything you find, but with that knowledge comes great ability to find ways to work with people you don't necessarily agree with all the time. Or, if appropriate, you might find ways to turn people around to your ways of thinking.

There's the kind of dance you can do in the middle where you hold onto your core values, but adjust enough to either adapt to someone who has a different style of working or help them adapt to you. You need to flex just enough to make things work with those around you who see the world differently, but not so much that you become brittle and feel forced to break your own values. The question to ask in any given situation is:

"Am I compromising, or am I being compromised?"

There's huge value and maturity in compromising for the good of the whole. But compromising to the point of damaging your most cherished values helps no one. Have this internal discussion with yourself throughout the year and look honestly at your leadership behaviors. Are you moving the needle, meeting people halfway, and helping to create a more productive and healthy workplace? Or are you letting yourself be dragged down by a toxic culture that you're unable to change, at least by continuing with your current methods?

Good things can come from conflict. But constant conflict with no positive results requires a change in approach.

TRIM TAB ADJUSTMENTS

One of the creative lab leaders at Google, Robert Wong, has a great illustration about the trim tabs on a boat. The trim tab works by lowering itself into the water at the back of the boat, creating a small amount of drag. Depending on its position and how far it extends into the water, it can quickly adjust the pitch or yaw of the boat. By activating a trim tab, the captain can adjust the angle of the boat, either to raise or lower the bow, or to prevent the vessel from listing slightly to one side, perhaps because of an uneven load.

What's fun about this mechanism is that it works on a boat of any size. Even the largest cruise ship can deploy trim tabs to correct any imbalance in the boat and keep the decks level for the passengers. Compared to the size of the ship, the trim tabs are relatively tiny, but they create a ripple effect that changes the whole orientation of the vessel and everyone on board.

Can you be a trim tab for your organization?

If you're trying to change an entire system of management, an ineffective culture, and the attitudes of everyone around you, you're going to be facing a constant battle that will drain you and leave you frustrated and defeated. But if, instead, you focus on your own sphere of influence, the people you're with every day, and do what you can to change things for the better, you can be your authentic self and have an impact on your immediate group. Over time, those positive moves you're putting into the workplace can ripple outwards and start to affect other groups, other departments, and even the entire company.

If a cruise ship is in port and you push against it with all your strength, you won't be able to move it an inch. But if the cruise ship is in motion, a comparatively small trim tab can make a significant difference. Don't worry about trying to change an entire organization through brute force. Be a trim tab and, in time, you may start to feel things leveling out.

GETTING UNDER THE HOOD

In the previous chapter, I talked about a favorite field trip, to the Rubin Museum, and how interesting it is to discuss the difference between your work being recognized as an individual or being recognized as part of a group. I want to revisit this subject for a moment because there is a marked difference in how people feel during and after the time they spend working on something that will result in individual recognition versus group recognition. The energy generated by those two different types of work can be quite different. They vary from one person to the next.

Some people thrive most when they receive recognition for their achievements, which means work they do as an individual is going to come with a lot of fire. This isn't necessarily an ego-driven position—although it can be. Sometimes it's simply that a person needs positive feedback to keep their self-esteem at a functioning level. Others don't like being singled out for praise or being the center of attention. So, for them, working on something that will be recognized as a group effort is a more comfortable and energizing mode of work.

As a leader, depending on which side you sit—and it may be somewhere in the middle—will affect how you organize and shape your team. Have a think about where you're most comfortable. Then, as a thought experiment, move yourself into the other camp and think about how that feels and how that would impact your management style. This is a useful exercise because, guaranteed, some members of your team will be on the opposite end of the spectrum as you and it helps greatly to know how they are likely feeling and responding to how their work is structured.

Where you and your team get energy is just one element of your individual team members' working preferences that you'll want to consider, but uncovering these nuances takes effort. It's the difference between individuals sharing thoughts, ideas, and resources with each other, and being truly aligned. Even assessment tools can only take you so far. To really dig into someone's thought processes and feelings you need to get under the hood.

The museum method works well because there are no easy answers to the questions it raises and it gently pushes people to look inward and then communicate what they find to the group. But this isn't the only approach. In truth, anything that takes people out of their "I'm at work" mindset can be effective.

RUBBER BALLS AND CHICKENS

Kevin Carroll, bestselling author of *Rules of the Red Rubber Ball*, has a theory that you can learn more about a person in an hour of play than a year of working alongside them. He'll literally bring a big, red, rubber ball (the kind you used to play kickball back in grade school) to a workshop and have everybody throw it around. Grown adults chasing after a red rubber ball is a sight to behold. But the ridiculousness of it has a fascinating effect on the energy of the room and removing social anxieties.

If this sounds a bit like an "ice breaker" exercise, you're not wrong. Except, first of all, I would never call it that because speaking the phrase out loud is enough to make most people clench from head to toe. Second, these are exercises I encourage you to try among groups of colleagues who have known each other for some time. It's not so much about breaking the awkwardness of being in a room with strangers as it is trying to get existing work colleagues to open up with each other and gain deeper levels of understanding. Third, many ice breaker games can be quite mundane—if you're planning to use "fun" as a tool for connecting people, be sure to choose an activity that is actually fun.

One of the games I have used in my workshops is called "evolution." I move all the tables and chairs so we have a big open space in the room and then everyone moves around the room playing "rock, paper, scissors" with each other. The catch is that initially, everyone has to pretend to be an egg. What does that look like exactly? Who knows. Everyone can decide for themselves what that means, but most people end up crouched down, waddling around the room, looking for someone to battle with.

If you win your "rock, paper, scissors" round then you get to evolve into a chicken. So now you're a chicken, hopping around looking for other chickens to challenge. Win that round and you become a dinosaur. Beat another dinosaur and you become a tree.

Yes, of course, it's completely ridiculous and the whole thing usually devolves into chaotic hysterics. But it gets everyone moving, gets the blood pumping, and for most people it lowers any social inhibitions they may have brought with them into the room.

Naturally, someone at some point is going to wonder, out loud, why the role-played evolution of the game is so odd. Going from an egg to a chicken has some kind of logic, but why a chicken into a dinosaur? And why does a dinosaur become a tree? At which point you can talk about how everyone's progress in today's workshop isn't going to be a straight, obvious evolution. It will have twists and turns, ups and downs, progress and regress. It's an odd way to make a point, for sure. But is it memorable? You betcha.

Do some people find this exercise uncomfortable? Yes, especially if they're more introverted. But to get everyone to open up during the course of the day, including those who naturally want to hide at the back, a little bit of discomfort is necessary. At least with this kind of game, everyone is in it together, rather than going around the room or putting people on the spot.

You're also giving people permission to be playful with each other. There's a reason close friends and family tend to joke and banter and be silly with each other. It's because there's a comfortable space between them that results from trust and openness. If you can invoke that in a small way through a fun exercise, whether it's throwing about a rubber ball or hopping around a room like a chicken, you're giving people room to relax and let their truest self emerge.

You can also, if required, use exercises to lower the energy in the room.

If you have a high energy group with a lot of chat and jokes, but you want to focus on something important and more thoughtful, it may well be in everyone's interests to slow things down a bit. If, for example, I'm about to deliver an important module on legal and compliance issues, as much as I love humor among a group, I probably want to tone things down for a more serious discussion. In which case, I might create a mindfulness or a meditation moment.

This doesn't have to be anything deeply spiritual—especially since this won't chime with everyone—but just a few moments of sitting quietly, eyes closed, feet on the floor, and helping everyone into a space where they feel grounded helps calm everyone. In that position I might talk everyone through a "body scan," inviting everyone to move their thoughts into each part of their body, from the feet up, noticing any tension in their back or their neck. Follow this with a few deep breaths, and once we're done the atmosphere of the room is noticeably more relaxed and peaceful.

Ultimately, it's about changing the natural work environment in a way that gets people into a different state of mind and, hopefully, ready to engage with each other. Sometimes simply taking people off site into a non-work setting can be enough. Or, if that isn't possible, take all the chairs and tables out of the conference room and get everyone to sit on the floor. Merely changing people's expectations of how things are going to unfold can be a powerful way to start.

When people come into a meeting room with pens and note pads, bottles of water on the table, and a slide projector all ready to go, people will assume a regular team meeting where we're going to go around the room and talk. Changing things up removes those expectations. And when your team doesn't know what's going to happen next, they have an open space in their mind that's ready for something new.

SEEING THE WORLD DIFFERENTLY

If your goal is to get people to think about how different perspectives can vastly change how people view the world while also encouraging thoughtful communication, try this exercise using the book *Zoom* by Istvan Banyai.

Zoom is a picture book in which each page shows a picture that is a zoomed out version of the previous one. It starts out with what looks like the top of a red, spiky hair cut. The next page is zoomed out to show a rooster (what you saw on the previous page was the top edge of the rooster's comb). The next picture shows a couple of kids watching the rooster through a window. The next reveals the kids are in a farmhouse surrounded by animals. And so on, until the final picture. I won't spoil it for you. There are lots of clever surprises along the way.

To turn this into an exercise, you'll need to cut out each page so you have each picture individually. You then give each person in your group one picture of their own that only they are allowed to look at. The group can discuss amongst themselves what they can individually see in their picture, in as much detail as they like, but they're not permitted to physically show it to anybody. The goal is to get everyone to line up in the order they believe their picture appears in the book.

It's much harder than it sounds. To complete the exercise successfully requires good descriptive skills, good listening skills, reasoning ability, and cooperation. Crucially, no one can hide at the back and let others do all of the work. Everyone has to participate to be successful.

It's a really enjoyable game and the potential lessons are endless. The obvious illustration is that sometimes, when we're working, we become so fixated on our own personal task we forget to consider how what we're doing fits in with the big picture of the rest of the team or even the organization as a whole. Wouldn't it be great if everyone developed the ability to zoom in and out of our own work and see how what we're doing connects with the grand scheme?

That's an excellent place to start.

RHYTHMS OF WORKING

I don't think anyone will be surprised by the concept that everyone has different preferences for how they work and how they can be most productive. It's obvious. Some people like to get up and start work really early. Others like to begin work later in the day. Some people are most comfortable integrating their personal and work life. Others like to keep those two things completely separate. Some people like to work in a noisy environment with lots of bustle and energy. Others like to put on their noise-cancelling headphones and be laser-focused on the task at hand.

But if this is so obvious, why is it so common for businesses to set strict limits on how and when their employees perform their work?

Some organizational structure is necessary, but there have been enough studies now for us to say, with a fair degree of confidence, that getting the most out of your team is best accomplished by allowing a certain amount of flexibility. The trend is to move in this direction with options such as flex-time and working from home. And if it's within your power to create that flexibility in your department or business, there are clear benefits to doing so, both in terms of improved output as well as the happiness and health of your employees. However, a word of caution: don't become so fixated on making your workplace the best place to be on the planet that you forget why you're doing it.

It sounds paradoxical, but when you're adjusting working parameters and rules for the benefit of your team, it's easy to fall into the trap of being overly prescriptive and actually reduce the flexibility your team members need to produce their best work.

This could manifest itself in a leader who, because they're intent on creating a culture with a great work/life balance, creates a rule that requires everyone to clock off at 5:00 p.m., regardless of deadlines, and go home to be with their family. On the face of it, this sounds like a thoughtful, bold policy. And it will probably go down well with most people. But what about the night owls who do their best work between 3:00 p.m. and 9:00 p.m.? Now they're having to push themselves to perform during a time frame that isn't comfortable. Or what about your single employees who live alone and would prefer to spend a bit more time with their work family rather than go home early to an empty apartment?

Setting a healthy culture that prioritizes health and family is an admirable goal. But it's usually best accomplished through personal example and empathy for those who need help adjusting their work schedule, rather than through fiat. Remember, employees are more likely to follow your example than your dictates. So, if you want your team to have a strong work/life balance, make sure you're visibly seen taking plenty of breaks, prioritizing family responsibilities, and keeping weekend work to a minimum. State clearly that well-being, in your department, is not just a tagline, it's an ideal. And encourage people to find their own way of managing their well-being and communicate that it's acceptable to develop a rhythm of working that is unique and effective for them.

The only time you may need to be a little more prescriptive is with regard to diversity. It's hard for an individual who is, in some way, different from most of the team to manage the challenges that come with that on their own. In this area, you need to be proactive. It might be as simple as having an "open door" policy for anyone who has a problem they need help addressing. Or it might require something more tangible. When I run training, I'm always keen to highlight that diversity is more than just gender and ethnicity; it's also neurodiversity and disability. For example, if someone on your team is hearing impaired, make sure your workshop or presentation videos have captions. If someone on your team has color vision deficiency, make sure your slides are comprehensible. If someone uses a mobility aid, be sure you don't arrange team activities that will unnecessarily exclude them.

This level of care for your team's comfort and ability to work effectively takes careful thought and a willingness to put in considerable effort. But leaders of all stripes recognize that this is a crucial part of the role.

SPEAKING THE SAME LANGUAGE

George Bernard Shaw once said that "England and America are two countries separated by the same language!" Like most good flippant quotes, it holds a lot of truth. Especially when we pair it with another quote from George Bernard Shaw, "The biggest problem in communication is the illusion that it has taken place."*

I see this all the time in the workplace. Because we speak the same tongue, there's an assumption that we're all speaking the same language and that everything we say is understood by the hearers exactly as we intend. This couldn't be farther from the truth. Our syntax may be the same, but the small nuances of language and communication that we picked up in the family

* It should be noted that the evidence for attributing these quotes to Shaw is limited.

home, from our close friends, from the schools we attended, and from our previous workplaces, all build up over time to create unique patterns of language.

These differences can usually be worked out over time through practice and experience, but there are ways to speed up this process and reduce the likelihood of miscommunication. As a leader and the developer of your work culture, you can affect this by popularizing and encouraging specific terminologies that would be meaningless outside of the office, but are rich in meaning to your team.

At Google, for example, we use something called "priority" language in which any task or project can be easily labeled to indicate its importance. It looks something like this:

P0 = Very Important and Urgent

P1 = Very Important but not Urgent

P2 = Important but not Urgent

P3 = Not as Important and not Urgent

Foundational = Regular, ongoing work that needs to happen consistently

Many organizations use some variation of the above, adapted to their world. It works because it creates a shorthand that everyone can understand, regardless of their specialism, and makes it easy to communicate where your priorities are at any given point in time.

If I say to someone that the particular task I'm working on is P0, everyone knows, without any explanation required, that this is going to take virtually all of my attention until it's done.

Initially this terminology was exclusively used by Google engineers, and other departments used their own methods of prioritization. But once this language spilled over and became universal across departments, conversations became noticeably easier. Why can't I work on this today? Because I have another task that's P0 right now. Why can't I get this thing I need from you? Oh, okay, it's because it's not P0 for you, so I understand that I'm going to have to wait.

It's such a simple set of expressions, consisting of only five unique phrases, but it makes a world of difference in so many different scenarios. Chief among them being that it changes the way in which people say "yes" or "no" to things they're asked to do. We all accept that saying "yes" to everything, all of the time is impractical and damaging. But we also hate to say "no" to things because we fear it makes us appear lazy or unhelpful. And, to be fair, saying "no" all the time isn't really an option. If a person or department consistently says "no" to requests then eventually people will simply stop asking, making the assumption that they know the answer before posing the question. But if people understand the reasoning behind your decision, this moves the conversation away from simply being positive or negative.

Context matters. And "priority" language can provide that without requiring lengthy explanations that, to the subject at least, can feel like excuses. It's a great relationship builder because it creates room for empathy without having to ask for it. Asking a colleague for help and getting a flat "no" is a world apart from asking a colleague for help and being told that they've just been landed with a P0 and they can't come up for air for at least a couple of hours.

From a practical point of view, it also invites the parties to find a compromise. If the help you need isn't available because of a P0 emergency, well perhaps you can assist with that P0 and allow both of you to get where you need to be a little quicker.

Language is communication, and communication is a flow of information. Working backwards, if we want a healthy flow of information in our business or department, a common language is the foundation. And, while it may not be immediately obvious, leaders have the ability to create that language.

BIAS BUSTING

If we have any sense of self-awareness, we acknowledge that we all hold some biases. Many of them may be harmless, but because they're usually unconscious* it's impossible to know for sure without taking the time to dig them up and challenge them. I am going to focus for a moment on a type of bias that most people overlook:

Our biases about ourselves.

There's a wonderful leader at Google called Marish. She came to us from another large corporation and she has a great picture of her at her first C-suite meeting. She's in a fabulous, tailored suit and high heels. The very image of the modern senior female employee in the workplace. But if you know anything about Marish, you'll know that this just isn't her. She was wearing what she thought she was supposed to wear, and acting in a way that she thought she was supposed to act, in order to get a seat at the table. She was the very epitome of someone who was not being their authentic self.

Marish went on a journey and is now unrecognizable from the corporate clone she initially presented. She leans heavily into her French heritage and runs around in fabulous sneakers. She is

* Or at least they should be unconscious. If we have conscious biases we should get rid of them immediately.

100 percent her cool, authentic self and completely comfortable with who she is and letting people see it.

The bias that began Marish's development was an unthinking assumption that if she was going to be successful in her career, she had to fit in with other people's expectations. Or, at least what she assumed other's expectations were—which is a whole other bias in itself. No one was being hurt by this bias. She wasn't mistreating anyone. But she *was* limiting what she was capable of achieving and was making the unfortunate assumption that people wouldn't approve of who she really was.

I see this conflict with a lot of people I coach, especially those in their twenties and thirties. There's an inner battle taking place between wanting to be authentic and wanting to be successful. And there's this assumption that this "real" person isn't going to be welcome and is going to hold them back. This is an assumption that needs to be tested. Because if you think being the "real" you is going to hold you back, try being a "fake" you that everyone instinctively knows is just a front. It's just not sustainable or healthy for the long run.

Think about all the times you've been to a summit or a convention and you've watched four different speakers in a row who might just as well have been the same person with slightly different hair styles. Same dark blue suit. Same plain tie with just a hint of color. Same polished-to-perfection PowerPoint. And then someone comes onto the stage in Nike trainers and purple hair and speaks from the heart for twenty minutes. It's a breath of fresh air that you'll remember for years to come.

I'm not saying that wearing smart suits and having well-prepared presentation slides is a bad thing. But only as long as it's the *real* you and not a performance. Being a leader in the workplace can't be cosplaying as Blake from *Glengarry Glen Ross*. You can't pretend to be something you're not because the authentic you will always be bleeding through. Far better to take off the costume and let people see what's inside.

This doesn't mean you can't change and grow. You must, of course, do both. But it has to be in line with your true values and your unique perspective. It has to be with the goal of becoming a better version of who you are, not what your unconscious biases are telling you you're supposed to be.

To be a leader is a privilege, but it's also an awesome responsibility. Your values are going to shape the culture and people who work in it. They're going to shape the careers and the well-being of everyone who works for you. Don't be fearful of this. Have a healthy respect for it and be bold with how you use this position.

Doing your best in leadership is something that is far easier to do when the pattern of values you're working from are your own—and a true reflection of your authentic self.

CARDS FOR HUMANITY

The Value Cards exercise, mentioned in chapter 1, is a powerful way to articulate your identity through core values. But you don't need the values written onto cards to complete the exercise.

Below is a list of 52 values and definitions (feel free to add more if the ones you really want aren't included). Write them out in the space provided below, placing each value under the heading you feel best represents your feelings toward it. Don't overthink it. Your initial, gut feeling is usually the correct one.

Once you've finished, if the "Most Important to Me" list has more than five words, narrow this down even further to the three to five values you truly care about; the values you absolutely could not imagine living without.

Your final selection gives you an insight into your authentic self. You've identified these values as the most important because they're so tied up with who you see yourself to be (or at least what you desire to be), that you wouldn't be yourself without them.

But simply identifying these values isn't enough. Usually this exercise is completed in a group setting because it's only by publicly selecting and talking about these values that they can start to drive how you live.

And, of course, how you lead.

If you don't have a group to complete this exercise with, an alternative is to share these values with friends and family and explain to them why they're important to you. This brings the values out of your subconscious and into your daily experience. And when you find yourself uncomfortable with a decision or experiencing conflict, think back to your chosen values and you'll likely find that one of them is bumping against something you're trying to do (or being asked to do).

You may also choose to create physical manifestations of your values to serve as a reminder to you, and to others, what you hold to be truly important. For example, one of my values is "Gratitude," so I had a pin created bearing this word and I wear it so I can literally carry gratitude around with me wherever I go.

It also reminds me to practice this value on a regular basis. Every time I get to enjoy sitting around the dinner table with my family, we take a moment to go around the table and give everyone the opportunity to answer the question: What am I grateful for today?

Think of it like an internal key performance indicator. Every so often, think deeply about your values, and evaluate whether or not you're being true to them, or if you're letting yourself be drawn away from your true self.

-Important to Me

-Less Important to Me

-Most Important to Me

VALUE	DEFINITION
Gratitude	To be thankful and appreciative
Curiosity	To be genuinely interested and inquisitive of the world around you
Equality	To promote what is right and opportunities for all
Excellence	To strive for greatness
Empathy	To be aware and caring of others' feelings
Balance	To keep steady and avoid extremes
Independence	To exercise free will and live life on your own terms
Integrity	To have strong morals; to do the right thing even when no one is looking
Belonging	To include and help others thrive
Resilience	To withstand or recover from challenges
Purpose	To live with intention and direction
Passion	To have an intense enthusiasm and desire

Order	To strive for structure and organization
Optimism	To find hopefulness in all situations
Pragmatism	To seek practical solutions to challenges
Uniqueness	To express your individuality and specialness
Mindfulness	To be present in the moment
Loyalty	To feel a strong allegiance to someone or something
Love	To treat others with deep affection
Leadership	To lead others; to be in charge
Justice	To promote fairness and equality
Kindness	To be caring and considerate to others
Ambition	To want achievement and success
Humor	To laugh and find amusement
Frugal	To be mindful of cost and not wasteful
Success	To achieve a goal or accomplishment

Stability	To need firm ground and consistency
Spirituality	To believe in something greater than yourself
Solitude	To need space and time away
Simplicity	To focus on essentials; to live with less
Daring	To be adventurous or audaciously bold
Responsibility	To have a sense of duty; to be accountable
Respect	To have regard for the feelings, wishes, rights, or traditions of others
Compassion	To have deep sympathy and understanding for others in need
Service	To do work that benefits others
Courage	To act with bravery
Creativity	To use your imagination or generate original ideas
Work Ethic	To appreciate determination and hard work
Education	To hold teaching and learning in high appreciation

Diversity	To appreciate differences in people and ideas
Family	To prioritize family over self and others
Connection	To focus on relationships with others
Environment	To show deep care for nature and the planet
Collaboration	To work with others for a common good
Fun	To be playful and have a good time
Authenticity	To be genuine and sincere in your interactions
Harmony	To strive for balance and calmness
Health	To promote mental and physical well-being
Growth	To seek continuous development
Honesty	To be truthful and genuine with yourself and others
Humility	To be humble and put others first
Adventure	To be up for new experiences

REFLECTION QUESTIONS: PATTERNS OF VALUES

- What are some of your positive traits you would like your team to imitate?
- What are some of your less desirable traits you wouldn't like your team to imitate?
- How would you describe the culture in your team?
- What would you like the culture in your team to be?
- What can you start doing (or stop doing) that might influence the culture of your team in the direction you'd like it to go?
- What contradictions are there between how you'd like your team culture to be, and how you act as a leader?
- How well do your instructions to your team reach the individual members?
- What changes could you make to your communication methods that will make it easier for your team members to stay abreast of your instructions?

- What does being a trim tab for your organization mean to you?
- What event could you create to help you learn more about your team's values?
- How much flexibility do your team members have to approach work in a manner that fits their individual modes of working?
- What biases might you hold that could negatively affect your abilities as a leader?

CHAPTER 4

PATTERNS OF STORIES

* * *

WHAT ARE YOU PUTTING INTO THE WORLD?

"Hey, Chris. How's it going?"

Chris slowed her stride but didn't stop. It wasn't that she didn't want to chat with her colleague, but she was two minutes late for a meeting she was chairing.

"Busy Super busy," Chris replied.

Chris and her colleague were walking toward each other, but once they met Chris kept going. She turned around and walked backwards so she could keep moving while apologizing so as not to appear rude.

"Sorry, we'll catch up soon. I'm running late for a meeting."

Chris's colleague, who had stopped walking, frowned.

"Are you okay, though? You look stressed."

"Yes, fine," Chris replied. "Just busy. Project deadlines. Kids wearing me out. The usual."

Chris gave a half grimace, half smile, to try and soften the words, but from the look on her colleague's face it wasn't having the desired effect.

Chris turned around to face the way she was heading and marched on.

Lisa McCarthy runs a workshop based on her book *Fast Forward*, in which she relates a similar story. Whenever she met someone and they asked how she was, the reply would always be something along the lines of…

"Busy."

"Super busy."

"Too busy."

"Tired."

"Exhausted."

"Worn out."

Or, often, a combination of the above.

But after repeating almost identical phrases several times in the same day to different people, Lisa was struck by a realization that, when they wrote her epitaph, it would probably read: "Here Lies Lisa—Busy, Tired Mom."

It's true, she was busy. And tired a lot of the time. You can't be a full-time senior executive and a mom without this being true. But those weren't the only things that described her. She was also excited by her work, proud of her accomplishments, and joyful over her children. And yet, when she replied to someone's greeting without giving it much thought, "busy" and "tired" were her stock responses. This is the story she was presenting to the world.

The more Lisa thought about it, the more she also became aware of the impact this was having on how others perceived her. The story that she was a busy, tired mom was only part of her tale, but it was the one that people had come to know above all else. So entrenched was this narrative, that people started reflecting the story back to her.

"I know you're really busy, but . . . "

"Are you able to help with this or are you too busy?"

"You must be exhausted juggling so many things—let me get you a coffee."

"Are you going to get a chance to get some rest this weekend? You must be exhausted."

Stories are powerful. They're the oldest form of entertainment. The best ones stick around for centuries. And they're a framework for how we describe the events and people in our life. But what we tend to forget is that other people are creating their own stories about us, based on how we present ourselves to them. Mainly through our own words.

The unfortunate effect is that often the story of our life that we have in our head is very different to the one that we've helped others to construct through our repeated expressions.

Is the story you're describing to people the story that reflects how you want to be known? Or is it a tale made up of instinctive, clichéd expressions that we express with little or no thought? Expressions such as…

"I'm not a techy person."

"I don't know what I'm doing."

"I always make a mess of that."

"That's not really me."

"I hate Mondays."

"I have no will power."

"I can't do that."

"Why do things always go wrong for me?"

"I'm feeling my age."

Say anything to people enough times and they will eventually start to accept this as reality. If you say, "Ugh, I don't know what I'm doing" repeatedly, even if it's in jest, even if it's just a self-deprecating half-joke to try to appear humble, others will eventually simply accept this as the truth. That you really, most of the time, don't know what you're doing.

And you know who else might start to believe these stories?

You.

When my daughter was doing her exam finals she was engaging in some horrible self-talk about not being good at math.

"I can't figure it out."

"I'm no good at this."

"I can't do it."

The last phrase, especially, was coming out over and over. What

I tried to communicate to her was that, even if she felt like she was struggling, let's at the very least modulate our language so we can talk about it differently. Instead of "I can't do it," how about "I can't do it yet?"

Henry Ford said, "Whether you believe you can do a thing or not, you are right." There's definitely something in that. Self-beliefs and self-doubts have a powerful effect on our ability to accomplish something and it often starts with the words we use or the words we hear. Did you ever have a teacher at school start out a new lesson by saying something like, "Trigonometry is a difficult subject so you're going to have to focus." The intention is good, but they're putting the idea into everyone's head that they should expect to struggle. How much better to say something like, "Right, if you really focus today you're going to find trigonometry absolutely no trouble at all. It's much easier than people say." You're mentally being nudged into a place where you expect to succeed.

Naturally, we want our team to succeed. Thankfully, science backs us in this endeavor. There's a rich vein of scientific studies about how our perception shapes our reality. From placebo drugs, to positive affirmations, to body language, when we intentionally absorb and communicate a belief or mindset, we increase the likelihood of it becoming a reality—both for ourselves and others. Our language is a huge part of that, and the impact can be felt by changing as little as one word in a sentence. "I can't do it," versus "I can't do it *yet*."

What impression do you want to leave people with? How do you want them to feel after you leave the room? Energized? Positive? Confident? Happy? Thankful? Peaceful? Something else?

It can be anything you want, but the key is to make a conscious choice and work at manifesting that through your words. If you don't make a deliberate choice, your subconscious will choose for you and although it might be something positive, it's just as likely to be something negative. It goes back to the values you've chosen to represent who you are and how you want to appear to the world. Select an impression that matches those values and you'll find it easier to use matching language, with the added bonus that you'll come across as more authentic.

Initially, you may need to be very deliberate in how you respond to certain questions and situations, but in time it will become automatic. Think about common questions you're asked, such as:

How are you?

How was your weekend?

How's your family/pets/friends?

How is your day?

How is your team getting on with <project>?

Next, think about some of the responses you might have typically given in the past and consider whether they align with your values. If not, or if there is room for adjustment, think about how you could answer differently.

Another method is to find a way to put your core value front and center so that you can easily remember to channel it in your interactions with people. As I mentioned earlier, I had a pin made containing the word "gratitude" so I have a constant reminder that this is the story I want to put into the world. Consequently, I need to keep shaping my words and my actions around this principle. You may find it helpful to do the same.

DON'T TAKE IT TOO FAR

One caveat to this goal of having your values enrich your language is not to become so locked into a positive mindset that you forget to consider your own needs. There's a fine line between relentless positivity and mindlessly accepting and putting up with everything that comes across your desk. Allowing wholesome, value-led language to become your story doesn't have to result in you being sidelined in your career aspirations—or taken advantage of.

Be mindful of this in your own work interactions, but extend this to your team members as well. Try and read between the lines of what people communicate in their language and how they might actually feel. And if you sense a disconnect, dig deeper to find out what is really going on.

Let's say you have a member of your team who is outgoing and sociable. They appear to be perfect for organizing team events, and when you invite them to do so they use language that suggests they're enthusiastic about doing so. But do they want to keep doing it all the time, or have they become pigeon-holed as the "social event" person and now feel like they can't object? You won't know unless you ask.

Or, even better, create an environment in which people feel secure and comfortable to come to you and say that, as much as they love a particular task, they don't necessarily want to do it all the time.

There are stories we tell about ourselves, and there are stories we write in our minds about other people. Some of those stories are accurate reflections of the individual, while some of them are not so truthful. Be mindful of the stories you're telling when you speak and make adjustments if you don't feel like they reflect who you are or who you want to become. Equally, listen to the stories other people are telling you, and be open to the possibility that there's more going on underneath.

LEADERSHIP STORIES

How can you tell if your most cherished value is at the heart of your authentic self? One way is to consider whether or not you have a story to tell.

Remember Geoff in chapter 1? He felt like "fun" was an important value for him, but when I asked him to relate a memorable time he had tremendous fun with his team, it was a real challenge for him. If you've chosen a value that is aspirational, rather than innate, you might also have a problem finding a story, but you should at least be able to think of an incident or a journey that is tangential. If your selected value doesn't come from a place of meaning in your life, you may need to rethink your choice.

If you're going to draw a line in the sand and say, "this is who I am, and this is what I stand for," it really helps to have a story you can tell. Not just because it provides that measure of authenticity, but because it helps those around you to really appreciate why it means so much to you. Stories allow you to communicate this in a way that no other technique can.

To give you some sense of what this kind of story might look like, I've asked some of the people I've worked with to share their own leadership stories. Some are tales of epiphany, in which developing leaders realized they needed to change their attitude or their management style. Others are examples of people using their value to overcome great adversity. What they all have in common is great openness about their own flaws and challenges. As you read these stories, notice how each one can be tied back to a specific value that the narrator either possesses or has developed, and that has helped them grow as a leader.

AMELIA EDDLEMAN
Director, Google Marketing Research + Insights

"I'm just going to be me . . . because I'm not very good at being anyone else."

Early in my management career I had an anonymous ethics complaint filed against me that claimed I discriminated against a team member by leaving a rude note for them. I was horrified.

An HR investigation confirmed that I consistently left handwritten notes for everyone on my team, all with the same matter-of-fact tone and typically without any pleasantries. It was determined that I hadn't done anything discriminatory and that there was no ethics violation.

But, in my view, it was certainly evidence of poor leadership.

Before this experience, I'd never thought anything of this practice. I left notes because I didn't work the same schedule as most people on my team, and I felt it was a simple way to communicate without having to call someone during their off hours. Unfortunately, what I'd completely overlooked was that some people read a lot of meaning into those notes, far beyond what I had intended. So, although I never meant any harm or rudeness, my intention didn't matter because I didn't communicate it one way or another.

When people have a lack of information, they make up their own story about things like tone and subtext. This is a human tendency we all have and one I'd greatly underestimated. I paid the price for that, and so did the people on my team whom I left guessing about my feelings toward them and sometimes feeling demoralized. The notes I wrote were reflective of my relationship with my team members—transactional. I had a high level of compliance, but no real commitment, and certainly not a pleasant team culture.

After some lengthy self-reflection, I noticed some important things about the way I was showing up at work. First, somewhere along the way I'd decided that to be taken seriously, I had to act seriously. Second, I prioritized tasks and results to the exclusion of everything else. As a result, I was behaving like someone I absolutely did not want to be. Who would want to work with an overly serious, task-driven jerk?

I'm grateful that this was early in my career and I had the opportunity to work with some really wonderful and fun peer leaders. Against my initial instincts, I decided to be very open with one peer in particular to get some feedback and input on what I should be doing differently. That person also knew me outside of work and convinced me that maybe just being myself, instead of Ms. Serious, would be completely acceptable.

It's genuinely funny to think back on what a novel concept this was to me at the time, and I was very uncomfortable for a while without my "stern" mask, but it was absolutely the right move. I changed my schedule around so that I regularly got at least some in-person time with everyone on my team, which mostly eliminated my need to communicate with people in writing. When I did need to do that, I made sure I added notes like, "Hey, I hope you're doing great today!" or "Looking forward to seeing you next week!"

It was a simple adjustment, but these communication changes and my mentality shift didn't just improve my relationships with my team members. I also enjoyed being around myself more.

Nowadays I can't imagine not prioritizing building trusted relationships with people at work or not being my authentic self. I think if you told my current team that I used to be really serious all the time, they'd have a hard time believing you. I joke that I'm just going to be me because I'm not very good at being anyone else. And thank goodness, because me being me is way more enjoyable for everyone.

NICOLE HUYNH
Google, Marketing Manager

"I feel most fulfilled when advocating for . . . the most underrepresented communities."

Defining my values truly changed the game for me. I know we've all done exercises like this before, but this one with Suzanne just hit differently.

Knowing and understanding my values changed several

things for me. The first and most noticeable change was that it was easier to receive feedback. I was letting the opinions of others really influence my view of myself and I would feel a need to convince someone that their feedback was inaccurate if I felt misrepresented. But once I was able to put words to my values I was able to filter feedback through my values lens—this meant taking in meaningful feedback from safe people, but also setting aside feedback that either didn't align with my values or didn't seem to come from a place of understanding of who I was as a person.

It also helped me manage my energy. I stopped spending time on things that didn't line up with the things that mattered to me most. I didn't put a lot of weight or give a lot of significance to things that weren't going to be aligned with my big picture and what mattered to me most.

But most of all, I figured out how I want to handle my next steps in my career. Being super clear about my values showed me that while I love what I do now and could probably enjoy it for the rest of my career, I realized I feel most fulfilled when advocating for and lifting up the voices of the most underrepresented communities. As a result, I have begun to put a lot of my time and energy (and 20 percent project work) into accessibility and DEI. My hope is to eventually turn my 20 percent work into a full-time role.

I'm so grateful for the leadership training I received from Suzanne and I couldn't be more excited to lean into the possibility of what's next!

MANSHA TANDON
YouTube, Marketing, India

"It's critical that people feel psychologically safe around me."

The most challenging piece of feedback I have ever received occurred while working at Google.

Over the past five years with Google people I have worked with have intimated that my tone is more instructive and aggressive, rather than collaborative. The toughest moment was when my previous manager and a close confidant told me that I was "not making a good first impression." He told me it was only after people got to know me that they became comfortable working with me, and that was unsustainable.

I was shocked, dejected, and angry, and I felt a visceral reaction, with my face heating up.

How could people think I am a horrible person and talk to my manager behind my back? Did they not appreciate the effort I was putting into my job?

Could they not see that I was a wonderful, kind, and compassionate person?

Did they not realize that my passion and drive was moving work forward?

But in time I realized that it didn't matter how I felt or what I thought about myself, or even what I said. All that mattered was how I showed up and made people feel. I've learned the hard way that communication and tonality is never about how you intend it, *but how the person at the other end receives it.*

Initially when tackling this problem I started to overcorrect, and found myself oscillating wildly to the other end of the spectrum—being totally unlike myself. I developed a tic (which I still have a little bit) of smiling constantly and breaking into a nervous laugh in the middle of a sentence, as if to somehow disarm or reduce the impact of a tough piece of feedback or a strong point of view. Sometimes—no exaggeration—I'd leave a meeting having smiled so much that my face would hurt.

But I couldn't sustain this inauthenticity for long. I couldn't even recognize myself anymore. So, I invested in myself and hired an experienced executive coach. I introduced her to my manager, who shared his perspective of me.

Over time, I've worked with my coach to understand how to:

- Influence more effectively
- Become comfortable with being my authentic self and sharing my stories, no matter how painful
- Be myself, but expand my range of behaviors
- Flex the different types of roles I can play in group settings
- Ask more, tell less, and practice deep listening

In all honesty, for someone who loves the sound of her own voice, the last item on this list meant sometimes vowing not to speak. For example, I contracted with my direct reports before going into presentations for them to pull me in when they needed me, but otherwise I would quietly observe. Installing that handy Meet extension that measures the percentage of time you've been talking has also been very useful*!

* https://bit.ly/talk-o-meter

From this experience, I learned that I want people around me to feel safe and comfortable. I want to be able to challenge the status quo, ask the hard questions, and demonstrate my passion for our company, our business, our products, and our users.

But to do this successfully, it's critical that people feel psychologically safe around me and incredibly comfortable when I do all these things. It is this learning that I will carry with me into future roles.

EDUARDO SAMUEL
Google, Group Marketing Manager, Global SMB Marketing Acquisitions

"I genuinely thought about how much I cared for them and wanted their success."

Feedback and coaching from those around me has helped me so much in my career. Whether from formal engagements, from work peers, or from friends from outside of work, it has always enabled me to slow down my thoughts and understand what's really going on inside my mind.

What often comes up isn't a reflection of work itself, but beliefs that I've held for a long time, or replaying situations that have nothing to do with my professional life.

I remember a situation with a direct report when I wasn't giving them the right feedback. I would lightly touch upon it, but I wouldn't describe the behaviors and the impact with the seriousness that they deserved. I realized that this had more to do with my desire to avoid conflict and to be liked than with doing the right thing for the business.

A coach reminded me of the gravity that I can bring to the room when I lead with my heart, and encouraged me to try that with this report.

I took a deep breath and went into a meeting with that report, trying to channel nothing but best intentions, and being as true to my feelings as I could. I genuinely thought about how much I cared for them and wanted their success—and I said those words while believing in them. Then I gave the uncomfortable feedback about the behavior and its impact.

It turned out that the feedback was only uncomfortable to me. What my report took away from the meeting is how much I cared about them, and vowed to change their behavior. Our working relationship only improved after that.

MAX JOSEPH

Google, Senior Marketing Manager, Operations

"This was my first experience with truly inclusive leadership."

When I first joined Google, I was hired as a Business Development Manager. I had never worked in sales nor did I view myself as a sales guy, so my first approach was to try to assimilate into this new culture—better known as "fake it until you make it." I changed how I dressed and how I talked, and I tried to mirror what I saw in "successful" Google sellers.

It was an abject disaster. I was unable to meet my performance goals and my client satisfaction numbers were average.

During a performance review, my manager could see that I was struggling to close my sales quota gap. She told me, "Stop. I did not hire you to be someone else. Being someone else is too hard. Just be yourself." Wow! This was my first experience with truly inclusive leadership. It was also the first time in my career that I had received such radically candid and direct feedback.

That moment, and that feedback, helped define two universal truths that I associate with being an effective leader. The first is that inclusive leaders encourage authenticity. People do their best work when they can bring the best of themselves to the office. As managers and leaders we should strive for work enculturation and not work assimilation. After receiving that feedback, I hung up my hard bottom shoes and Burberry pants in favor of jeans and sneakers. I never looked back.

The second is that every failure has a teachable moment. What a remarkably liberating insight! What my manager taught me in that moment is that failure is a learning and growth opportunity. Not only did I take her feedback to heart, I also increased my risk tolerance. I was more comfortable within the team and pitched for revenue opportunities with my clients.

REFLECTION QUESTIONS: PATTERNS OF STORIES

- What message or attitude are you putting into the world when you interact with work colleagues?
- What story can you tell that reflects your most cherished value(s)?
- Which stories from other leaders (either from this book or from your personal experience) most resonate with you? Why?

CHAPTER 5

PATTERNS OF HIGH-PERFORMING TEAMS

* * *

HOW MUCH DOES ENVIRONMENT MATTER?

One of the key reasons for Google's success comes back, again, to its reliance on data. When you have a company the size and scope of Google, you have the ability to uncover fascinating trends and what connects the best-performing teams across every discipline.

By now it shouldn't surprise you to learn that the markers of a high-performing team can be defined in terms of values and how well they are distributed through their culture.

FIVE KEYS TO A SUCCESSFUL TEAM

A few years back, Google's People Operations team* carried out a two-year project to answer the question: What makes a team great?

They interviewed over 200 Google employees across over 180 teams, and considered over 250 individual attributes. What they hoped, or perhaps even expected, to find was a perfect formula of personality traits and abilities that, when represented within an individual team, would give it the best chance of success. Kind of like trying to figure out the perfect sports team by having the perfect mix of size, strength, and ability all mixed into one perfect group.

It turns out that didn't exist.

What actually made a team successful was not so much about who was on the team, but how the members interacted with each other, how they structured their work, and how they viewed their contributions.

This was a hugely significant finding because the implication is that virtually *any* team can be successful if they are simply organized in an effective way.

Let that sink in for a moment.

As the leader of a team, you have the ability to make your team successful. Not by trying to assemble the perfect mix of employees—shuffling people in and out—but by managing your team to allow them to work under a specific set of dynamics. If

* At Google, we refer to Human Resources as "People Operations" (which I love, by the way).

you're a manager in any capacity, and this information doesn't make you sit up and take notice, then nothing will.

The research group identified five key dynamics that were common to the most successful teams at Google. I'm going to quote them here exactly as defined on the re:Work website*.

- **Psychological safety:** Can we take risks on this team without feeling insecure or embarrassed?
- **Dependability:** Can we count on each other to do high quality work on time?
- **Structure & clarity:** Are goals, roles, and execution plans on our team clear?
- **Meaning of work:** Are we working on something that is personally important for each of us?
- **Impact of work:** Do we fundamentally believe that the work we're doing matters?

I'm not going to go through all five factors because re:Work already has a huge amount of information, freely available.† But I am going to talk a little bit about the first item on this list: psychological safety.

If you'd asked me before the project began which quality would be most indicative of a successful team, I probably would have said something about communication or organization. But psychological safety turned out, far and away, to be the most important factor. In fact, that trait is the foundation of the other four. If you don't have psychological safety, the likelihood of your

* https://rework.withgoogle.com

† I suggest starting with https://rework.withgoogle.com.

team enjoying any of the other dynamics is close to nil.

The short description of psychological safety, as outlined above, is about feeling secure in what you're doing. For example, have you ever been in a meeting and temporarily zoned out, only to realize you missed something important? Do you feel comfortable and secure enough to speak up and say, "Sorry guys, I missed that last part, can someone please catch me up?" Or do you keep quiet and hope nobody asks you any questions about what they just discussed?

If it's the former, you're experiencing a high level of psychological safety. If you're in the latter, it's very much the opposite.

There are other examples that illustrate the difference between psychological safety and its opposite. Let's call it psychological anxiety:

- You're in the middle of a project and you feel unsure as to what the overall goal is. Can you ask someone for clarification or are you too concerned that you'll look like you don't know what you're doing?
- You're asked to do a job that you feel unsuited for. Can you ask for some assistance or training, or are you too afraid that you'll look weak?
- A workplace event conflicts with your religious beliefs. Do you feel confident that you can ask to be excluded without judgment or do you decide to just call in sick?
- You make a critical error in your work. Are you comfortable owning up to it and asking for help to put it right, or are you more likely to attempt to cover it up?

As a leader, you probably don't have any of those concerns unless it involves your interactions with your own manager (if you have one). But for every single member of your team, these are real challenges they face on a regular basis. In every case, the best decision for the well-being of the individual and the team is obvious, but how confident are you that every member of your team will make the right choice? The answer is a measure of how psychologically safe your team feels.

FEEDBACK, FRICTION, AND SANDWICHES

It's not just the leader of a team who needs to be able to give feedback. Every member of your team should, at various points, be able to give feedback to each other, whether it be to tell someone that they've done a great job or to explain why their performance is not good enough. But giving feedback is outside of most people's natural expertise and the tendency can be to just avoid it altogether and rely on you as the leader to pat people on the back or point out their mistakes.

This is not conducive to a close-knit team that respects and trusts each other, because without positive feedback from each other, no one really knows whether their teammates value and appreciate them. And without the negative feedback, not only do people fail to recognize their faults, it can also give rise to harmful grumbling gossip behind people's backs.

You don't need to create a formal mechanism for encouraging people to give each other feedback; as long as you have a healthy culture of open dialogue, this feedback will happen naturally and your team will learn to appreciate that they're never left wondering whether they're doing great or falling short. However, there's more involved than helping everyone feel comfortable speaking their mind. Because there's no question that people respond to feedback very differently depending on who it comes from and how it's delivered.

When it comes to feedback I've always been very pro-sandwich, meaning that if someone needs to draw my attention to an error I've made, I prefer that it come in between two positive pieces of feedback. That doesn't necessarily work for everyone—some people prefer just to hear bad news directly without any preamble—but I believe that any feedback is going to be more impactful when it comes from someone you trust and admire, and who respects your personal needs. This means the only way to ensure healthy, meaningful feedback between everyone in your team is to help them develop those close, respectful connections.

There's a real benefit to being able to take feedback from anyone—even someone you don't like—and accept it on face value without being put off by who it is delivering the message. But that's a rare skill. Most of the time, when we get feedback from someone with whom we don't have a strong connection, it's just going to bounce off us and be quickly forgotten. But the other extreme is also true: the *more* we like and respect the person giving us feedback, the more likely we are to take it very seriously.

How can you engineer this respect in your team? How can you help them build those empathy and caring muscles so that, whether they're giving or receiving feedback, the experience is a positive and meaningful one?

Some of it comes down to culture and your example as a leader. Are you showing yourself willing to give feedback when it's needed without shying away from it and without doing it in a way that makes people feel bad? Are you willing to accept feedback from members of your team without being high-handed and pulling the seniority card? Are you making it obvious that errors are not something to be afraid of, and that feedback is simply a way of helping everyone grow and develop in their abilities?

That's part of it. But mostly, it's about engineering comradery among your team. Going out for a meal together, taking a field trip, attending a work event, arranging a team-building exercise, or any other methods you can think of that put your team together in a close-knit environment, outside of the office, allowing them the opportunity to put aside their work armor and show their authentic selves.

Because when people see their team members from different angles, and observe that they have abilities that they might not have the opportunity to display themselves in the workplace, everyone becomes more three-dimensional. Feedback and open conversations are invaluable for a group of people who work together day in and day out. You should encourage this transparency, not just through your own example, but by helping everyone on your team to forge lasting, meaningful connections.

Ultimately, sharing feedback is about how comfortable your team is in speaking their mind and being their authentic selves. If they have concerns about how they'll be perceived or that there may be negative consequences, people will self-censor and then everyone suffers. In many teams the leader sets the tone that "this is what we're going to do, keep your opinions to yourself, and just do what you've been asked." This is not only unpleasant for people working under this kind of regime, it also inhibits individual team members from showcasing the best of their talents.

DIVERSE PERSPECTIVES

We must go back, again, to the subject of diversity. Aside from the value of making people of all stripes feel welcome and have opportunities, having a diverse team allows you to hear different points of view, discover different, more effective, ways of doing things, and to identify potential problems that a homogeneous group might miss. But that diversity will be totally wasted if your team doesn't have a high level of psychological safety. Those distinctive voices will be silenced by fear.

High-performing teams are able to have tough discussions, say unpopular things, and be their authentic selves because observation and experience have taught them that, even if doing so causes temporary discomfort to themselves and others, everyone benefits in the long run, and no one is vilified for speaking up.

Creating that environment of psychological safety is very much in your hands. It either exists or doesn't depending on the culture you've developed and how you respond to friction or challenges within your team. It's not a case of degrees; you either have safety or you don't. And it's definitely not something that will happen by accident. Your natural leadership qualities may lend themselves well to this type of environment, but even if you have the foresight to tell people that speaking out is welcomed, your team won't fully believe it until they see, on a regular basis, people demonstrating that they can speak openly without negative ramifications*.

Depending on how your business or department is structured it may also be important to take a moment to consider: who exactly is my team? There are your direct reports, obviously, but what about your peers? Or what about other teams that work closely with yours? There might be finance partners, legal partners, HR partners, temp workers, and/or agency workers. It's an important question to ask because you need to be absolutely clear that, when you use the word "team," your team knows exactly who you're talking about.

Your definition of "team" sounds like it should be obvious,

* For more on this subject, I recommend watching Amy Edmondson's Ted talk: https://www.ted.com/talks/amy_edmondson_how_to_turn_a_group_of_strangers_into_a_team

and from your perspective it might be, but that won't necessarily hold true for everyone else. In your mind, your team might be you and your direct reports. Simple. But it's likely that you're actually part of other groups and, maybe without even realizing it, you have your own hierarchy of priorities that makes your posture less clear to everyone else. It's possible that your direct reports are your number one priority, and everything else slots in somewhere directly below that. But teams are usually more complicated than that.

Thinking about how you spend your work time and where you put your energies reveals far more about what you believe your team to be than anything you might say. It's important to know where you stand when it comes to prioritizing your energies or resolving clashes in scheduling. Essentially you're challenging yourself with the question: Who is your *primary* team? Is it the team of your direct reports with you as leader? Or is it the team in which you have a more subordinate position with your manager as the leader? Where does your loyalty lie, first and foremost?

It's a tricky question to answer and there isn't necessarily a right or wrong response. But it's important to know because the truth in this area will color how you talk to your teams, the promises that you make, how you divide up your attention, and how you structure your days and weeks. Your team members will notice all of these things and they will mentally and emotionally position themselves accordingly.

I heard a story about a British gentleman in a senior position at one of the Big Five banks who had arranged an annual team-building event. But the leader of that department decided not to attend because she had important work that needed completing. I'm not judging her decision—no doubt she was under pressure from her manager—but it's not hard to see how this will be viewed by the team she leads. In their minds, it will seem that her role as part of the senior management team takes priority over her role as leader of her team.

There's no easy answer to this one. Unless you're the owner of the business, you will be part of more than one team and you have no choice but to make decisions about who takes priority at different moments. But you do need to have some sort of answer, even if it's just to acknowledge the current state of play and decide if you need to tinker with it. However you decide to structure your hierarchies in your mind, it's worth noting that, if you want your department to feel psychologically safe, they need to feel that they are your priority more often than not.

YOUR MISSION, SHOULD YOU CHOOSE TO ACCEPT IT . . .

Jessie was in a pickle.

Her 360 degree feedback was pretty awful and confirmed what she'd suspected for some time —her team was very unhappy. People were reporting feeling burned out, not cared for, and, worst of all, unclear about why what they were doing mattered. Which, you may recall, is the exact opposite of the fifth dynamic of a high-performing team.

Jessie, to her credit, took this seriously and arranged for everyone to take a couple of days out of the office to collaborate and come up with a new set of values that would define the team going forward. The goal was to produce a mission statement that everyone could agree on and that would change the whole mood of the office. By the end of the workshop they had a beautiful manifesto that everyone was convinced would change things for the better.

But when the plan hit the real world, it fell apart very quickly.

The intentions of Jessie and her team were good, but the mission statement, as powerful as it was, couldn't change the fundamental reality of the nature of the business. In practice, the team was performing a type of crisis management. Clients would come to them with urgent problems that needed rapid, intense resolutions. And that meant often working on weekends or staying late on weekdays. The very nature of the work didn't lend itself to the ideal of prioritizing work/life balance or setting rules around nine-to-five schedules.

It was a bit like the emergency department at a hospital getting together and creating a mission statement built around the notions of not taking on too many patients and having regularly scheduled coffee breaks. It's an unrealistic mission and it's going to fall apart the moment it meets with reality.

We'll come back to Jessie a little later, but her example neatly illustrates that, although mission statements are important, there's a lot more to creating a successful version than simply taking every team member's desires and compiling them into a memo.

A mission statement, a vision statement, a values statement, whatever you choose to call it—and yes, I appreciate that they're all subtly different—is about helping your team appreciate why they exist, what they do, and how they go about doing it. These are fundamental questions for helping a team to believe that what they do matters. So, whichever type of statement you decide to create, it's important to have something that matches up with the type of work you do and that is actually meaningful to the people who work under it.

That sounds like an obvious point to make, but the whole reason why mission statements have become something of a cliché is because they frequently rely on fuzzy, abstract aphorisms that look nice on first viewing but don't hold up to scrutiny.

One of my previous employers had their mission statement in big letters on the wall as you entered the building. And yet, if you'd stopped me in a corridor while I worked there and offered me $100 to repeat it, I wouldn't have had a clue. It was a nice piece of marketing, but it didn't have any impact on my day-to-day work. I looked it up to refresh my memory and, even now, I struggle to fully parse the phrases used. Apparently the company innovates "every day," which sounds great from the outside, but for the people who work there that sounds like a recipe for chaos. Or, at the very least, permanent exhaustion. They also list "joy" as one of their values. Again, this sounds lovely, but does this reflect the experience of the average employee there? Maybe it does. Maybe every department is overflowing with cakes and smooth jazz. But I have a suspicion that this statement is more for the investors than it is for the workers.

I urge you to move away from creating your mission statement for the wrong audience. Don't make it about the customers or the shareholders, but make it about inspiring your team to work with purpose and enthusiasm. If you work at a very large company, it will also be helpful to create your own department-specific mission statement that takes into consideration the work that your team performs. Company-wide mission statements for businesses with tens of thousands of employees almost have no choice but to become fairly generic. But there's nothing to stop you, as a leader, from creating your own carefully crafted version that sits alongside the company line.

I frequently get asked to run a workshop to help a team create or refresh their mission statement. I appreciate these occasions because I believe that involving the team in the process is really important. When everyone has played some part in whatever the final statement looks like, they're more likely to adopt the values within and understand what the desired effect is intended to be. That said, I would advise against trying to involve too many people in the process, at least in the initial discussion. Five people is ideal, but certainly no more than ten.

I usually start by pinning down exactly what we are creating:

Mission Statement: What you do now. Why does our team exist?

Vision Statement: What the team is aiming to achieve in the future.

Values Statement: What the team cares about. How do we operate?

Those are very loose definitions, and a good place to start, but in truth it can be anything the team decides is most appropriate. Even the terminology can be customized. I've had teams refer to their creation as their "north star," "guiding principles," or "manifesto." The exact wording is less important than being clear from the outset exactly *what* it is they're setting out to create.

The next stage can be one of the most challenging because you're often beginning with a blank canvas. One of the tools I like to use is a deck of cards that contains a series of abstract images that are very much open to interpretation. Each person in the room picks one card that they feel reflects the current state of the team and another that depicts what they'd like the future state to be. Then everyone takes some time to explain their choice. The images on the cards aren't really important, but it gives everyone an opportunity to express themselves and get some ideas out there.

Another method is to get everyone involved to complete a short questionnaire before the workshop and then I use the results to create anonymized word clouds that I print out and stick onto the walls of the conference room. When the team shows up for the workshop, they can walk around the room and place sticky notes next to the words or phrases that resonate with them and the ones they don't like for whatever reason.

Once you have a good collection of values and concepts, you can start to whittle them down to those which seem to be the most popular with the most people. But the goal isn't to reach a final decision by the end of the session. The project is too important and too complex to complete in a single day. My goal with these initial workshops is to get some really good discussion going and a good sense of what is and isn't working.

After the workshop, one person volunteers to take a stab over the next few days at creating the statement (or statements, if the goal is to create separate mission, vision, and value versions). Everyone involved provides their feedback and the statements can be modified accordingly. It usually takes at least three iterations before you have something that everyone can get behind. And, crucially, something they feel they can properly explain to others.

I try to steer teams away from falling into the trap of trying to include everyone's ideas so no one feels excluded. It's a laudable goal, but it's too easy to wind up with something that is just a mess of contradictions and semicolons. The person responsible for condensing the ideas into something meaningful should be capable of wordsmithing the results into something concise but still purposeful.

The final creation should reflect the feelings and ambitions of the majority but it isn't going to satisfy everyone completely. That's the nature of producing anything by committee. Nevertheless, you can help your entire team embrace the mission statement by continuing to do work around it. Once a year it's good to get everyone together and talk about the mission statement and how it measures up to reality. If there's a disconnect, does the team need to do more work to adjust working styles and attitudes, or is it the statement itself that needs some more work?

No mission statement should be set in stone. It isn't something that you want to change with every variation in mood and feeling, but you should be open to making adjustments if it's clear that what you've created isn't suitable.

Remember Jessie, who created a mission statement that was abandoned almost immediately? She didn't give up on the idea, but she did stop pretending that their work wasn't, by its very nature, stressful and hectic and inconvenient. That wasn't something that could be changed, so the mission statement would have to take this into account. In the end, Jessie created an ethos built around the idea that, when a tough project was underway, everyone would be super-focused and support each other in getting the job done, even if it meant long days and canceled plans. But when there were gaps in between projects, the team put an equal amount of focus on regrouping, resetting, and rejuvenating, and getting mentally and physically prepared for the next round.

It couldn't be pedal to the metal 365 days a year, but it also couldn't be a steady, gentle pace every day either. When they were working hard they worked hard, and when they were resting, they rested hard. That inclusion created a more realistic tone for the mission statement.

Interestingly, this realization also inspired an adjustment in Jessie's hiring methods. From that point, job descriptions and job interviews made it very clear that this role was *not* a nine-to-five gig. It was an all-out sprint for the duration of a project, and then a recovery period before the next challenge. This allowed Jessie to attract people into the department who were excited by this style of work, but exclude people who might come in with unrealistic expectations around what the workflow would be like.

Don't let anyone tell you that mission statements are pointless or just for show. High-performing teams have clarity on why what they're doing is important, and why they're doing things the way they do. A well-defined mission, vision, or value statement that is frequently referenced and reviewed—rather than just being a poster on a wall—can give your team lucidity and purpose.

CHAPTER 6

PATTERNS OF RESILIENCE

* * *

CAN YOU FILL THE CRACKS WITH GOLD?

"I'm sorry, Alice, the promotion isn't going to happen right now."

Alice didn't say anything, and her face was impassive, but I could see the cogs and gears whirring in her brain behind the façade.

"You're doing well, and you've got a great career ahead of you . . ." I continued.

"Hang on," Alice interrupted me. "I don't understand. I've done everything that was asked of me. What did I do wrong?"

"You didn't do anything wrong," I said. "The role scope isn't there and the timing isn't right."

"What does time have to do it? I worked non-stop to get this promotion. You know I did. You can't just brush me off with 'not the right time.'"

"I'm not brushing you off," I said gently. I was trying to stay calm, but Alice's control had slipped and it was clear she was feeling very angry. I'd prepared myself for this moment and thought about how I would respond differently depending on whether her reaction was one of upset or annoyance. But I hadn't prepared for just how irate she would be.

"Well, then what was it?"

I hesitated. I didn't mind Alice being angry with me. It was an understandable reaction. I wanted to tell her all the details to try to help her recover her dignity. But I also had a duty to my managers and my peers, and it wouldn't be appropriate to reveal details about sensitive conversations that had taken place. There were, unfortunately, larger business considerations than Alice's career that she wasn't privy to. And I realized that, even if I were to explain this, it was unlikely to make her feel any better about the situation.

"What?" Alice demanded again, her demeanor way beyond anyone's reasonable definition of insubordinate.

"Well, then you should have fought harder for me. I really feel like I should have gotten this. You made out like you were backing me and… it's not right."

"I know it's frustrating."

"I can't…" Alice stood up, her whole body trembling with frustration. She tapped her knuckles on the table between us and looked at the door to the meeting room; a fight-or-flight battle going on in her chest. "I can't talk to you right now. I'm going to say something I regret. I need to go. I need… I think I need to go on leave for a bit. I need a break."

Alice left the room and, to her credit, she had enough composure not to slam the door behind her.

KINTSUGI—FILLING CRACKS WITH GOLD

I broke Alice a little bit that day. It wasn't intentional and I'm not even sure it was avoidable, but it happened.

So, I had two choices. I could bristle at her anger, allow a rift between us to grow, and then gradually drift apart. Or I could help her repair the damage and use this as an opportunity to help her heal and become something new and formidable. That's where Japanese ceramics come into play.

In fifteenth century Japan, shogun Ashikaga Yoshimasa's favorite Chinese tea bowl was broken. He sent it back to China to be repaired but it came back stapled together with metal pins and he was unhappy with how it looked. As a result he tasked Japanese craft workers with coming up with a new method of ceramic repair that looked more pleasing.

The result, a practice that has survived to this day, came to be known as "kintsugi," meaning "golden repair." What is definitely true is that the art of repairing broken vessels with a gold-infused lacquer has survived to this day.

Ceramics repaired using the kintsugi method have a distinct look. They appear to be whole and functional, but the spiderwebs of gold that reveal where the vessel was once damaged give it a beautiful, unique appearance. What's interesting about this process is that, whereas most ceramic repair work sets out to be as invisible as possible, kintsugi goes in completely the opposite direction, making the repairs the most visually noticeable part of the entire design.

The philosophy that has grown around kintsugi centers around embracing imperfection and impermanence, as well as the idea that breakages healed makes the whole more distinctive and more beautiful. It's a stunning metaphor for what happens when we endure a damaging experience but recover to become something totally unique and special. But what I love most about this philosophy is the idea that we don't need to hide our former cracks. They're a part of our history and they made us what we are today. Instead of covering them over as if they're something to be ashamed of, we can celebrate them as part of our journey to how we got to where we are.

I had a similar choice to make regarding Alice. How would I address those cracks? It took a couple of weeks for her to cool off and let me back in. But once she returned, instead of chastising her for not being more professional, I showed her, through my actions, that I held her in high esteem and that she was important to the company—and me. I arranged multiple one-on-one sessions to show her how invested I was in her career progression. Gradually, over time, we filled those cracks with gold and she is now one of the leads on my team. Ironically, the promotion, at the time of writing, hasn't happened yet. It will. I've no doubts. But in the meantime, Alice is developing into something really special.

Would it have been better to avoid the breakage in the first place? You might argue that. I could have been more closed off in my encouragement and praise so her hopes weren't raised so high. I could have tried to lower her expectations by making it sound like reaching the next stage of her career was probably too difficult for her.

Avoiding disagreement and friction is easy. All you have to do is keep your head down, don't engage with people, and avoid all opportunities to connect with the people you work with. Maybe Homer Simpson was right: "You tried your best and you failed miserably. The lesson is, never try."

But would Alice be in the strong position she's in now? Would she be excelling in her role and making herself stand out as a future leader? Or would she be somewhere in the middle of the pack, getting on with her work quietly, and never putting in that extra effort to develop her abilities?

A poor leader ignores the people on their team with strong potential simply to avoid the possibility of disappointment and conflict. And when those disagreements and upsets happen—and they will happen—it would be even worse for a leader who treats those people as disposable, rather than striving to help fill those cracks with gold.

Gold or trash? It's a choice. And it's an easy one. It's just that carrying out that decision takes patience and effort. But it's worth it. Absolutely worth it. When teams go through the crucible together, they bond and come out stronger on the other side. As a leader, you simply need to have the resilience to take the long-term view. In the tense moments there'll be tears and cross words and impulsive actions that people will probably regret later. And yet, if you can see past the emotions of the moment and show a waiting attitude, even the most broken vessel can be restored to something more beautiful than ever.

GOING OVER THE CLIFF

We settled her into the basket and tried to make her as comfortable as possible. She was so afraid she was shaking, but we all knew it had to be done.

Next we strapped her in, and tied ropes to the basket. The tension in the group was incredible and I'm sure we were all thinking the same thing: "I can't believe we're actually going to do this."

We checked, double-checked, and triple-checked the ropes to make sure everything was as secure as we knew how. But we couldn't put it off any longer. We maneuvered the basket to the edge of the cliff and sent it over the edge. The basket swung under its own momentum for a little while, and only once it had stabilized did we begin to lower it, as gently as we could manage, down the cliff face.

This may sound like the result of a mountain hiking event gone awry, but it was actually a team-building challenge—although admittedly quite extreme. Here were our instructions:

> *One of your team members has been badly injured and is losing blood. The only way for them to survive is to get them to the bottom of the cliff, using the basket and ropes provided, where a helicopter and paramedics are waiting. The injured person is losing blood at the rate of one pint every ten minutes. If they lose five pints of blood, organs will fail and death is almost certain. This means you have just 50 minutes to get the injured team member to the base of the cliff using the equipment provided.*

Obviously, there were professionals on hand to make sure we were doing everything safely, but that didn't stop the challenge from being a particularly hair-raising one that most of us didn't know was coming. The first job was to decide who was going to play the part of the victim.

A lady on our team volunteered. She had a fear of heights which you would probably assume made her the worst candidate, but just being on the cliff was stressing her out and she just wanted to get down as quickly as possible. I felt bad for her because she was genuinely terrified and shaking. But, wow, was she brave. Not just to put herself forward, but to actually go through with it.

With the time limits and the intensity of the exercise, you don't really have time to think about how this is subsequently going to help you as a team. But afterwards, when you take the time to debrief, the teaching points come quickly. There are plenty of moments in the office, when you're under pressure to perform, when you have to go over the cliff together. And you're only going to be successful if you're capable of figuring out who is best-suited to each role and then working together, trusting each other, to get the job done.

The stakes aren't usually as high as life and death, but when the pressure is on it helps to know that you're capable of supporting each other to reach your goal, even if it means doing tasks that take you out of your comfort zone.

Whether or not you want to take your team through such an intense exercise is up to you, but in terms of bonding a team together I've never experienced anything quite like it. It's been twenty years since that day, but I would still be able to pick every member of our team out of a crowd. We went over a cliff together.

BUILDING RESILIENCE OVER TEA

Google considers resilience to be so crucial in the workplace that they literally have a team focused on resilience. Their job is to run consultations and training courses to help Google employees deal with work-related stress and operate at their best. One of their activities is called the T.E.A. Check-in, designed to help individuals (or teams) pause and reflect on their regular habits and routines and identify areas that might need adjusting. It covers three simple topics:

THOUGHTS

Today my mind is…

To refocus I need to…

ENERGY

Today my energy is…

To change or maintain, I need to…

ATTENTION

To be my best today, I will focus on doing or being…

I really like this exercise as something to do along with your team. It encourages mindfulness, but more importantly it allows everyone to learn more about their colleagues, where they're at, and what challenges they're facing.

It can actually be tremendously encouraging to do this short exercise together with your team and for someone to find out that they're not the only one feeling low energy today. Or that they're not the only one struggling to focus because of a personal challenge. The "we're in this together" mindset is a powerful one and resilience is always stronger when people have the support and understanding of those around them.

I also recommend using longer team meetings as an opportunity to cultivate resilience and help your team manage stress, especially if you've recently completed an intense project or a long spell of overtime sessions. Pfizer and Google both refer to these events as "off-sites" (which is slightly misleading since they often take place in the office) and they take place two to three times a year. Resilience exercises can be built around a specific task, such as a business review or a training update, but this T.E.A. Check-in can then be wrapped into a longer meeting that doubles as a team-building event.

Team building, workplace bonding, staff development—whatever you choose to call it—has a poor reputation in some quarters. Usually because people have had bad experiences at events that were poorly managed and offered little in the way of benefits, but sometimes because they're viewed as an excuse to put down tools and avoid working for a time. Don't be put off by this. A well-run, well thought-out event can be hugely encouraging for your team. And while the financial and productivity benefits of the connections and bonds that are created between your colleagues can't easily be measured in a tangible way, there's no question in my mind that a close-knit team is more likely to be a high-performing one.

Recall that "psychological safety" and "dependability" are two of the five characteristics of a high-performing team, and team building can go a long way to cementing these two qualities in your group.

Don't let a busy work schedule get in the way of this. If you put aside a day for your event and you have a lot of essential business to cover, leaving only an hour for team-building activities, then you haven't put enough time aside. Creating bonding moments for your team shouldn't be viewed as something you can tack on the end for a little extra boost. It's a wasted opportunity and your team is unlikely to put much effort into participating if it's clear that you haven't put much effort into the preparation.

Ideally the business element of the meeting and the community side should be given equal time. And if that means you need to schedule a longer meeting, then so be it. Alternatively, take a good look at your agenda and consider whether everything needs a lengthy segment. Can some of the items be delivered in a pre-meeting brief, followed by a brief summary on the day? Or can some of the items be removed entirely and just communicated by email?

Avoiding the trap of trying to cram too much into the agenda (my rule of thumb is no more than one topic per two to three hours) also allows the business side of things to double as a team-building experience. By allowing some breathing room around each topic, it puts less pressure on you to rapidly monologue your way through the material, and affords opportunities for your team to participate and discuss the subject as a group.

A gentle schedule also gives you the freedom to set longer breaks and longer lunches, which is a great venue for your team members to eat and drink together and forge those valuable bonds. Remember, for many members of your team, this meeting is a well-earned break from their hectic schedule, and they won't thank you for hosting an event that is itself a frantic rush from morning to evening. A slower, more relaxed timetable is more conducive to learning and remembering the content, and creates space for your team to communicate in a stress-free environment.

I appreciate that this may be a different approach to these types of events, but I encourage you to try and see for yourself how much everyone gets out of the experience. And I do mean "see for yourself." I've known team leads who outsource these meetings to an external vendor because they felt they were too busy to do the event justice, but this sends a terrible signal to the rest of your team. The optics look like you're too busy for them. Your team likely contains future leaders and if you pass off your coaching and mentoring to someone outside of your organization you're teaching them it's acceptable to be hands-off in this process. By all means use other managers and leaders within your organization to assist you, especially if you know people internally who are especially skilled at teaching and inspiring future leaders, but it makes no sense to try to divorce yourself from this important element of your responsibilities.

Resilience is a team sport and you're the coach. So, do your part in building this characteristic in everyone around you.

CONFLICT RESOLUTION

My father is a retired U.S. Army colonel and so, for him, turning up to an appointment on time was to be late. I didn't realize how much this perspective had rubbed off on me until I began working at Google and I found myself irritated at the majority of people turning up to meetings either right on the dot, or five to ten minutes later.

What was the best response to that? To challenge people directly about their lack of punctuality? To try to shift the culture so that lateness became unacceptable? Or perhaps just bottle it up until I became resentful and grumpy with people who didn't show up on time?

Maybe something else.

Let's imagine for a moment that one of your team members is habitually late arriving to the office in the morning. You're not happy about it and so now you've got to deal with this situation. There are lots of options available and some of them are more advisable than others. Let's work through a few of them and

I'll highlight a few opportunities you might have to resolve the situation with a minimum of fuss and without harming your relationship with the employee in question.

First of all, make it a habit to tackle issues as soon as possible after they occur. No one likes being pulled up on something they did a month ago that they can barely remember. A swift resolution also reduces the likelihood of a problem escalating.

But that doesn't mean you should react impulsively. Tackling the person immediately without any forethought is going to see you running hot and less able to access your empathy and patience. At the very least, give yourself a minute to take a deep breath and be open to having a conversation about the problem, rather than the interaction just being the form of a "telling-off." If your employee is late into the office for the third time this week and you've decided enough is enough, marching them straight into a meeting room while you're still feeling the irritation is setting up a scenario that could end badly.

Now that you've taken a pause and given yourself room to think, run through a few questions in your head.

- Am I viewing this as a problem because I think that leaving it unaddressed will hurt this person's career or damage the team in some way, or is this just a personal annoyance?
- If this is just a personal irritation, do I really need to take action to try to change the person or the team, or will it be more beneficial to everyone if I changed *my* attitude toward this issue instead?
- Do I believe that this person is capable of making the needed changes or is this the core foundation of who

they are? If it's the latter, can I change something in the environment or in our working practices to accommodate them better?

- If I decide to talk to the person about this issue, am I in the right frame of mind so I can talk to them without irritation or judgment, and do I have a clear idea in my mind of what change in attitude or behavior I'm hoping for?
- Am I going into this meeting with an open mind, ready to listen to this person's side of events?

The last item on this list may be the most important because, no matter how much you may feel this is a black-and-white issue, there will always be details you don't know and can't predict that can change the perspective entirely.

When you're speaking to your tardy employee, it may feel like an obvious, straightforward infraction—everyone else arrives in the office at 9:00 a.m., and this person arrives at 10:00 a.m. But they might tell you that they were under the impression that their contract was for a set number of hours, and that they generally stay at least an hour later than everyone else in the office. So where's the problem?

Maybe they add that their mom's really sick and they drop her off at the hospital several times a week so it really helps to be able to start work a little later in the morning.

If you come into this meeting with an accusatory attitude right from the outset, the employee might not tell you any of these things and simply agree to be "on time" in the future, leaving the meeting upset and frustrated. Or, if you're so fixated on what you've already decided is the right solution, you could miss the opportunity to help this person and support them through a difficult period in their life. Maybe flexible working hours is actually the best thing, not just for this employee, but for the rest of the team as well. Or, if not, perhaps you could seek permission to let the rest of the team know that this employee needs to work a different shift a few days a week to support their family, so no one feels like you are offering any undeserved special treatment.

There are lots of possible outcomes here, but open-mindedness and empathy gives you access to far more solutions than a rigid attitude that is focused more on rules than people.

Things won't always go smoothly. Real life doesn't guarantee happy endings. It might turn out that the person is just disorderly and lacking commitment to their role, in which case you may have no choice but to make your expectations for their future actions clear and warn them that disciplinary action may result if they don't improve.

Sometimes, whether you like it or not, conflict is going to be unpleasant and cracks are going to appear. And on occasion, the damage will be so great that repair is impossible. Resilience can help you here as well. When a relationship with an employee is damaged, you can seek to fill it with gold, but if this isn't feasible and you have to let the person go, it's important to recognize that this is the reality of a leadership position. If you're resilient, you won't let such events discourage you from reaching out to help and guide other members of your team.

Resilience finds its worth in the team lead as well as the team as whole. And, much of the time, its strength in this area will be a reflection of your own.

REFLECTION QUESTIONS: PATTERNS OF RESILIENCE

- What does your personal kintsugi vessel look like?
- Which members of your team could use your help repairing their cracks with gold?
- What steps are you taking to build resilience?
- When can you arrange your next "off-site" meeting?
- How could you improve how you deal with conflict with your team members?

CHAPTER 7

PATTERNS OF CONNECTION

* * *

CAN YOU PRIORITIZE YOUR ATTENTION?

I checked my watch for the umpteenth time.

Usually, when I'm hosting a workshop and the attendees are talking, I avoid looking at my watch. It feels impolite and gives the impression that I'm not interested in what they're saying. But on this occasion the stress was threatening to get the better of me.

The workshop was in its final stage and we were set up in a gratitude circle. Everyone was granted the opportunity to share their final thoughts and express what they most appreciated from our sessions. Typically this exercise takes around an hour, but today everyone had a lot to say and much they wanted to share. We were now well into the second hour and it was looking increasingly like I was going to miss an important call with my boss. I wasn't relishing the idea of letting down the manager, one of the most senior members of staff in the company.

There was the option to say, "Hey, I'm really sorry but we're running way over time and I have an important meeting to attend." I doubt anyone would have taken offense. But it would mean cutting someone off, as well as denying other people in the group the opportunity to speak.

I've run many of these workshops and I will hopefully run many more. But for this group, it might have proven to be their only chance to have this meaningful experience. To halt the exercise early would be to prioritize my anxiety over their opportunity to create an inspiring memory. I would definitely disappoint people in the present to avoid potentially disappointing people in the future. Even if one of those future people was my manager, would that be fair?

I sent a quick "SOS" to my team to let them know that I was potentially going to miss my meeting and would need to reschedule or that someone would have to attend in my place. Once I'd done that I quieted my mind and told myself: "Be where your feet are."

I'd literally just been talking with the group about leadership and the importance of being present in the moment. What kind of message would it send if I then immediately bailed on everyone? So, I stayed and gave everyone time to share their thoughts and feelings about the journey we'd just taken together.

The world didn't come to an end. As busy as her schedule was and as demanding as I knew her to be about setting high standards in the workplace, I trusted that she would understand my absence. And I also trusted that there were other people in the meeting who would communicate what I had hoped to and would champion the initiatives I had hoped to weigh in on. Yes, the missed meeting came with a cost. But the reward was that this group had a beautiful closing session and I had the privilege of being a part of that event.

"JUST A SECOND, MOMMY"

Connecting with people, for most of us, is hard. It's messy. And it costs us emotional energy. But there are arguably few things more worthwhile. The human experience is one of the great adventures of our lifetimes, and it can't exist without other people colliding with each other in wonderful and unexpected ways. This is all the more important when you consider how much the march of technology has interfered with our natural ability to bond with the people around us. I don't want to be the hundredth person to remind you that being focused on your phone to the exclusion of opportunities to talk with our friends and family is harmful, but I'm going to do it anyway.

Connecting with people is crucial for our mental and physical well-being, but it takes a conscious effort. And in the age of smartphones, tablets, laptops, and televisions, more exertion is needed than ever.

Some years ago, when my daughter was about three years old, I tried to talk to her and she responded by raising an index finger in my direction and saying, "Just a second, Mommy." I recognized the phrase and the hand gesture immediately because, I realized, this was exactly what I did when she was trying to get my attention and I wanted to finish writing an email or finish reading a paragraph before I was interrupted. It was unpleasant to see her mimicking my mannerism, and it hit me hard to think that it probably wasn't much fun for her to be on the receiving end of it either.

That led me to the conscious choice to attempt to be more mindful about giving her my attention when she needed it, and not subtly making her feel like she had second place in my priorities. Being successful in this meant being more present in general, but especially around my children.

It's not easy to take up the challenge of being more engaged with the people around you. The pull to constantly check our phones isn't just about YouTube and social media, it's about pressure from work, demands from family, deadlines to meet, and people you don't want to disappoint. But learning to balance the external demands for your attention with your efforts to connect with the people physically in your vicinity is one of the best gifts you can give yourself.

A study in Canada in 2012* discovered that people who made an effort to smile and talk to their barista reported improved mood and a stronger sense of belonging. Additional studies since then, in a variety of countries, have confirmed these results, finding that even when people feel dread at the idea of talking to strangers, when they make the effort to do so they experience greater feelings of happiness, optimism, and empathy.

This all feels intuitive and almost obvious. But if so, why do we struggle with it so much? Because, again, we come back to that ever-present battle between disappointing people in our vicinity and disappointing people elsewhere. When I was torn between potentially upsetting my manager or potentially upsetting an

* https://www.bbc.com/future/article/20221026-why-talking-to-strangers-can-make-us-happier

invested group of workshop attendees having an amazing day, I went back and forth in my mind between the potential outcomes. But in the end, it wasn't difficult to figure out the right choice. It was only the execution that was challenging.

The worst-case scenario for me was a ding to my reputation. And yet, even though this was possible, I didn't think it was likely. If I was constantly canceling meetings with senior staff, then this could have been the proverbial straw that broke the camel's back. But, I'm generally reliable, so I trusted that any damage would be short-term and limited, and I could smooth things over if required. The correct decision was clear and, once I stopped hedging and settled my mind on what I intended to do, the anxiety went away and I became fully present.

I pondered on whether there's a formula we can use to decide which connections to prioritize. Is there a pattern we can observe that makes it easy to figure out how to settle conflicted attention? I'm not convinced that there is, because every rule you could come up with will have its exceptions. As a general guide, however, I think there are two factors that will make decisions easier.

1. **Hierarchy of priorities:** Family, friends, customers, direct reports, peers, and managers all demand and deserve your attention. If you're clear in your mind the order in which these people take priority in your life, you can decide who wins when there's competition for your focus.
2. **"Here" trumps "somewhere else":** If you're torn between two different connections and you're not sure who deserves the greater attention, I don't think you can go far wrong by prioritizing the people who are in your physical space.

These two elements don't remove our obligation to make the hard choices, but at the very least they can help us avoid instinctively prioritizing our devices, which is rarely the best option.

WHEN PEOPLE TALK, LISTEN

One of the most dispiriting results of 360 feedback is when people find out that the people around them don't feel connected to them. Or, worse, that they feel like the person doesn't care or isn't interested in others. That's a harsh truth to learn.

When this happens, the first thing I point out is that this report isn't *the* truth, it's *a* truth. It's a single datapoint in a snapshot of time. And just because you're *perceived* to be a certain way, doesn't mean you *are* in fact that way. It may simply be that you're not letting your qualities show as you would want to. If connecting with people is not a natural strength, that's okay because it's something you can learn.

This doesn't mean you have to force deep, meaningful relationships with everyone at your workplace. That isn't practical or even desirable. But if you can improve your connections with even just a few people this can have a ripple effect where you're not just in a better relationship with those in your immediate circle, but you're presented in a more positive way to others by the people who know you best. You can deliberately choose the people you want to forge closer connections with, if that's your preference, but in practice it's far better to let it happen organically by being more engaged with people in general and letting deeper relationships emerge.

My father was a master at this, I think instinctively, because he was always 100 percent in the present. When you talked to him you sensed that he was giving you his full attention and that he was genuinely engaged with what you had to say. This is a tremendously attractive quality because, frankly, we're all flattered and encouraged when someone takes a genuine interest in us. It's a sad thing to realize, but most of us rarely, if ever, experience the pleasure of having someone talk to us and genuinely want to know who we are and what we think. So, when it happens, we instinctively warm to that person and naturally open up.

It's simple enough to write down: be present and listen to what people are saying. But it takes practice, especially if we're the kind of person whose brain is always racing and finds it hard to focus on just one thing. For most of us it will be a learned skill rather than a natural ability, but all it requires is repeated, conscious effort for it to gradually become instinctual.

When people talk, listen. Don't think about what you're going to say next and don't worry about how you're going to keep the conversation going. *Just listen.* If there's a natural break in the chat, ask the person a question about themselves and, again, listen to their response. Make it clear you're listening by using body language and vocables. Don't let your mind wander to the past or the future. If you catch yourself doing this, mentally bring yourself back to the present, a practice that will eventually become a habit.

Once you learn to do this well, you'll discover that people will warm to you in a way you may not have thought possible. Especially when, on the surface of it, you're doing nothing more than listening and being present. Your genuine, undivided attention is a wonderful gift you can give to others, but it's also a gift to yourself. When you realize that you're exactly where you need to be in that exact moment, and you don't need to rush off somewhere or hurry the conversation to an end. You can start to appreciate the joy of just taking a few minutes to do nothing but connect with someone. With enough practice you'll find that even a brief two- to three-minute conversation can become a moment of real meaning that can make another person's day.

ASK THE RIGHT QUESTIONS

A good opportunity to practice your blossoming connection skills is the empty space in the 10-15 minutes at the beginning of a one-on-one meeting (or the 10-15 minutes before a group meeting begins), when you're making small talk about the commute or the weather or sports. Instead of relying on your favorite, mostly meaningless, chitchat, try encouraging the person to talk about something meaningful to them.

I could give you a stock list of questions to ask, but I don't think that would help you in the long run. It's far better for you to think about what you know about the person, regarding their family or their interests, and ask them something on those topics. This demonstrates that you care about this person enough to know and remember something about them, and also invites the person to share something important that you're going to listen to with genuine interest. Feel free to get really intentional with this. I literally write down the names of people's spouses, children, pets, and hobbies, so I can remind myself of some great topics to bring up when we meet.

For example, my teammate Sabrina wrote a wonderful fantasy book called *The Botanist*. This is a passion for her and it's wonderful to see her light up and describe the stories around it. The amazing thing is that this even works with people who are naturally quiet. If you can figure out what they care about most and encourage them to share, even the shyest of people can become avid talkers.

Do, however, be careful about using closed or self-serving questions. It's not that they're inherently bad, but they won't have the same effect as open, curious questions. Remember, the purpose of these conversations is to connect and demonstrate that you're interested in the person, not to show off what you know or how good you are at solving other people's problems. When I'm running a peer coaching workshop I often challenge the attendees, for the first round at least, to only ask questions, specifically "what" and "how" questions. "Why" questions aren't allowed because they're usually in service of the coach's curiosity and not the coachee's well-being.

For example, if someone tells you they're having trouble sleeping, "Why aren't you sleeping?" is the obvious question, but it jumps straight to the conclusion and makes the conversation a fact-finding exercise. Better questions might be, "How is that affecting you?" or "What solutions have you tried?"

I also recommend avoiding "red herring" questions in which you try to sneak your wisdom into the conversation by disguising it as a query. "Have you tried melatonin?" sounds like a question, but really it's just me saying, "You should try melatonin." When someone has a health problem they've probably already tried many different solutions and they're probably sick to death of people immediately diagnosing them and telling them what they should do, with only a cursory understanding of their circumstances. So when you, instead, show genuine empathy and compassion, and attempt to understand what this person is experiencing, rather than making it about your ability to solve the problem, you're opening yourself up to forging a real connection.

At the risk of sounding repetitive, don't lose sight of the fact that a conversation with a person with whom you're trying to connect needs to be primarily about that person. If someone has a sick parent or partner, lots of people will be asking them about the ailing person and how they're progressing. And that's a perfectly nice thing to do. But I can guarantee that hardly anyone, or maybe no one at all, has then gone on to ask that person how *they* are coping with the situation.

The reverse of this is also true. When someone asks you a meaningful question, you have an opportunity to connect with that person by giving them a meaningful answer. You don't have to share anything you're not comfortable with, but opening up to other people, even in small ways, can prompt them to do the same. If you think back, you can probably still remember random conversations with work colleagues from years ago, brief as they may have been, precisely because one or both of you shared something personal. For a moment in time you made a connection.

All of this might feel like a lot to remember, but actually most of it will happen automatically if you remember to be present and genuinely interested in the other person. It's why I can't give you a stock list of questions to ask. Your desire to connect with someone has to come from a place of authenticity or it will immediately fall flat. Or worse, appear to be manipulative. Your interest must be real, and therefore so must your questions.

TRULY CARING ISN'T A "HACK"

Many years ago I interviewed for a job, and the interviewer commented that my clients seemed to really like me. She wanted to know my secret. I responded, almost without thinking, that I genuinely cared about them. The interviewer's response was one of confusion and almost distress. She didn't seem to know what to do with that answer. I think she was hoping for a technique or a script. Something that could be templated and packaged and taught to interns. She genuinely seemed baffled by the idea that caring for my clients could be authentic.

Saying that I succeed when those around me succeed has become such a banal phrase, adopted by so many on social media who want to signal their virtue, and yet it's a real concept that exists when you truly care about the outcome of your relationships. But it can only work if ego and self-interest are removed. The moment it becomes seen as a "strategy" or a "technique" it loses all power.

This might feel like a paradox because I'm literally describing this to you as a method you can use to build connections. But intentionality in this area is perfectly fine as long as you let go of that in the moment by being fully present when you're making that connection. That's the difference. If you try to connect with people as a means to your own ends and you never let go of that thinking, even while conversing with others, you cannot, by definition, ever be fully present.

When I walk into a workshop or a coaching session and I'm thinking it has anything to do with me, then I know that I'm not in the right headspace and I need to do something about it. Now.

Or if I'm listening to someone talk, but I'm thinking about what I want to say next, then I know my focus is wrong and I need to shift it back to the person in front of me.

Once you can give someone your full, undivided attention, you really can't go far wrong. Even if your attention wanders briefly—a perfectly human thing to do—you can bring yourself back to the moment by saying to the person, "Okay, here's what I think I heard you say.... Am I understanding you correctly?"

Don't be alarmed if you don't make a success of this practice overnight. It will come to some more easily than others. But never doubt that this is worth the effort. Connecting with people is one of the few essentials in life that cannot be outsourced, cannot be delegated to a junior, cannot be managed by technology, and cannot be replaced with solo activities. Interpersonal relationships, when nurtured, improve every aspect of our lives, including in the workplace.

But it's down to you to make it happen.

Isn't it ironic that most of us spend more hours of our free time being entertained by movies and TV shows that simulate personal connections between fictional characters, and all the joys and tears and excitement and revelations that result, than we do enjoying those experiences in real life with the flesh and blood people in our lives? Is that a pattern worth changing?

REFLECTION QUESTIONS: PATTERNS OF CONNECTION

- Do you have any habits relating to prioritizing technology over those who are physically present?
- How would you rate your ability to truly listen when people speak?
- How would your team members rate your ability to truly listen when people speak?
- What conscious efforts can you make to forge better connections with people in the workplace?
- What opportunities do you have to practice and develop your connecting skills?

CHAPTER 8

PATTERNS OF LEARNING

* * *

CAN YOU ESCAPE YOUR RIVERS OF THINKING?

When you're a hammer, everything looks like a nail. Or, in my case, when you're a learning and development specialist, everything looks like a learning opportunity!

I'll freely admit my bias, but I think I can make a good argument that leaders who maintain a learning and growth mindset perform better and have greater career longevity than those who have a fixed way of thinking. I've seen plenty of leaders who are very, very good at what they do, and as a result they have a "stay in my lane" attitude. That tends to result in them becoming extremely successful in one specific area, but I don't see many being promoted to more senior positions or getting anywhere close to the C-suite. For that type of career progression you need to expand your abilities outside of your current field of vision.

Being comfortable in your position isn't always a bad thing, and we'll revisit this subject later in this chapter. However, developing patterns of learning is an absolute requirement if you're going to make intentional moves in your career and in your development as a leader.

And that requires curiosity.

I could have, in fact, called this chapter "Patterns of Curiosity," because, to my mind, "learning" and "curiosity" are virtually synonymous. And there's no better place to direct your curiosity than at your own ability and willingness to learn and develop. Here we come full circle, right back to our very first chapter on "Patterns of Self." Developing the ability to continually learn begins by looking inward and asking whether you're demonstrating that drive in practice, or if all of this is just between the ears.

Ask yourself:

- What have I learned, if anything, in the last three to six months, either about myself or about skills that go beyond those required for my current role?
- If I were to ask my team and my peers about my attitude to learning, would they describe me as a keen student and an advocate for personal development?
- When I learn something new, do I excitedly share it, or keep it to myself?
- Looking at the last major project I completed, have I taken the time to reflect and consider what I learned during the process?

- If I schedule personal time for learning and development, is it focused on new abilities or simply on doing what I do better?

The last question in this list is particularly interesting because it's always easier to train in something you enjoy and in which you already have some abilities. It's good to lean into your strengths, but it is possible to take this too far and become locked into one specialism—the aforementioned "stay in my lane" approach. Again, specialization is fine if this is what you want your career to be about, and you're doing this intentionally, but just be aware that this won't be as helpful as you might imagine when it comes to progressing into more senior roles. If that matters to you then I encourage you to pair your curiosity with a certain level of flexibility.

One senior leader, John, delivered a talk recently in which he described becoming fascinated by Artificial Intelligence (AI) and doing a deep dive into the subject. Not just reading a few articles on the subject or even the abstracts on research documents, but reading the full papers, eating all the levels of detail, learning the language of the field, and immersing himself fully in the science. He described the experience as enjoyable but also humbling. When you've been at the top of your main expertise for so long and this forms the basis of your job, going into a brand new subject where you're a complete novice and starting from scratch forces you to remember just how little you know in the grand scheme of things.

John is an expert in many different areas, but he found diving into something completely new incredibly stimulating and refreshing. Taking in huge swathes of new understanding and going from zero to 60 in a matter of weeks was a real palette cleanser from the normal experience of already being an expert and only very occasionally adding something new to his knowledge.

You don't have to dedicate weeks or months or your life to learning something new if that doesn't appeal to you. It certainly won't help to learn for the sake of it. But if you find yourself curious about something that sits outside of your normal patterns of learning, embrace it and see what happens. It doesn't have to be a lengthy or formal study session. Maybe you stumble across something that piques your interest and you decide to go down a YouTube rabbit hole and watch a bunch of videos on the subject. That willingness to learn will serve you well, not only in terms of expanding your knowledge, but also in helping you to become more flexible and adaptable. Which, in turn, opens you up to a longer and more varied career.

There's a concept in building and architecture called "design flexibility*" in which buildings are specifically created with the idea that, in the future, they might need to serve a completely different purpose. An office space today might later become a hotel. Or a hospital might become a shopping mall. Although this isn't a particularly new idea, it's become a growing trend, in part, because it's more environmentally healthy to adapt an existing building than it is to knock something down and start over. In practice, this might take the form of using open-plan structures that can be easily repurposed, or designs that allow walls and ceilings to be easily removed to change the shape and height of the space.

In the same spirit, I'd like to coin a concept called "development

* https://www.the-possible.com/the-ultimate-flexible-building/

flexibility," defined as a mode of thinking that favors learning new things and is open-minded about changing long-held methods of working. This mental flexibility has served people well in the past (every new technological breakthrough has been dominated by the people quickest to embrace them), but all the more so now in an era where change is arguably more rapid than at any point in human history.

John's AI journey is a good example because, at the time of writing, AI is one of the most commonly discussed commercial subjects on social media and news websites. Some are excited by it, some are terrified by it, some are deeply skeptical of what it can achieve. But if you're a flexible learner, instead of rushing to judgment—either for or against—you can take some time to look below the surface and see what's really going on. This may or may not help you in your current role, but if you've let your curiosity guide you and performed even a little research, you'll be in a strong position to weigh in on the subject if it does eventually encroach on your working environment.

This is another reason why I believe people who lock themselves into a single discipline tend to be overlooked when it comes to moving into more senior roles. Focusing on one skill almost to the exclusion of everything else inhibits your ability to be agile and adapt to the times. No leader at or near the top of a business lasts for long if they're stuck in their ways and can't shift their mindset—as well as the mindset of the people they're leading.

Even if you feel you are well equipped for a high level of flexibility, you must still maintain an intentionality in your efforts. Human beings are very good at finding shortcuts in their thinking without even realizing it's happening.

COACHING, CONSULTING, OR COUNSELING?

Coaching is a growth industry and the range of specialties seems to expand daily. There are business coaches, life coaches, career coaches, team coaches, health coaches, leadership coaches, spiritual coaches, finance coaches, and more.

Basically, whatever challenge you're facing, the chances are good that there is a coach out there who specializes in that particular subject.

I believe this is a good thing. A really great coach can be a powerful force for good in your life. Unfortunately, *finding* a great coach is never easy. There are a lot of mediocre coaches out there and, sad to say, quite a few poor ones. There's also a certain amount of chemistry involved. A coach could have a long list of blistering endorsements, but for you the experience might wind up being uncomfortable and leave a bad taste in your mouth.

Finding the right coach involves a certain amount of trial and error, but there are a number of things you can do that will speed up your search:

1. **Be clear on the kind of help you're looking for.**

The best coaches function a little bit like mental health counselors. They ask great questions and are incredible listeners. And they're not just absorbing your words, they're also taking in your tone and your body language to get a deeper understanding of what it is you're saying, and also what you're not saying that needs to be drawn out. They can also hone in on inconsistencies in things you share to help you get to the truth about how you really feel about a situation.

On the opposite end of the spectrum are coaches that act more like consultants. They'll listen to your challenges and, rather than coaxing you to develop your own solution, they'll simply give you specific advice.

Other coaches sit somewhere in between these two styles.

The problems arise when you're looking for one type of coach but wind up with something completely different. If you're hoping your coach is going to draw you out and uncover your unspoken mental blockers, but their style is simply to give you advice, this is going to be frustrating for both of you. Even more so when you're looking for direct advice and all you're getting is more questions.

It would be helpful, in my view, if people differentiated themselves better between being a coach or a consultant. But in practice you're going to have to do your due diligence and discuss a prospective coach's style and consider whether this is going to be a good fit for what you need.

2. **Consider whether you want an industry expert or an outsider.**

Most of the time you'll likely want a coach who understands your industry, but there may be occasions when it's better to work with an outsider.

If you're new to a particular niche or if you're still expanding your knowledge, a coach with experience and expertise in that area is going to be invaluable. Even if you're an expert yourself, a coach with a strong level of knowledge is going to be able to help you figure out how to best channel your efforts. It's a little bit like a world-class tennis player using a coach who, as you would expect, doesn't play tennis as well as the professional. But the coach has the experience the player needs and an understanding of what it takes to physically and mentally prepare the athlete for their next match.

On the other hand, if you're at a high level of experience, but feel that your methods are stagnating, working with a coach who doesn't know your industry can bring a fresh perspective and help you find ideas and strategies that an insider would never imagine. If you have very deep rivers of thinking, working with someone who doesn't have that limitation can be an amazing way to get you out of your rut.

So, too, if you're fairly new to an industry but want to be competitive in your own way, without walking the same furrowed path that everyone else walks with predictable results. Again, a coach from outside your field can be invaluable for finding fresh directions.

3. **Have a set agreement for the desired outcomes.**

It's common for people to put themselves in the hands of a coach and trust them to create and run the agenda. As tempting as that approach can be, I always recommend being involved and having an agreement with your coach around how long the relationship is going to last, what the plan is going to be, what the long-term objectives are, and how the coach is going to approach your sessions.

This comes back to whether you're looking for coaching, consulting, or something in between. Setting out the expectations that both of you are going to have (your coach may want specific commitments from you with regards to your participation), from the outset, will give you the best chance of achieving your desired outcome.

There is no one who is so intelligent, so emotionally secure, and so self-aware that they can't benefit from having a coach. If this is a path you want to explore, I encourage you to go for it. But don't jump in feet first without taking the time to find the right solution for your specific needs. People, for example, often ask friends or colleagues for a recommendation. And while there's nothing wrong with that, make sure you consider the above before making your selection. Just because a coach did an amazing job with someone you know and trust doesn't mean they're the right choice for you.

ESCAPING YOUR RIVERS OF THINKING

Author Edward de Bono, inventor of the phrase "lateral thinking" (no joke, look it up), developed a concept in one of his books, *Lateral Thinking: Creativity Step by Step**, called "rivers of thinking."

* https://www.goodreads.com/author/quotes/6980.Edward_de_Bono?page=2

A landscape is a memory surface. The contours of the surface offer an accumulated memory trace of the water that has fallen upon it. The rainfall forms little rivulets which combine into streams and then into rivers. Once the pattern of drainage has been formed then it tends to become ever more permanent since the rain is collected into the drainage channels and tends to make them deeper. It is the rainfall that is doing the sculpting and yet it is the response of the surface to the rainfall that is organizing how the rainfall will do its sculpting.

That's some juicy metaphorical prose. We could spend an entire book unpacking that beautiful passage. But we'll stick with the most obvious interpretation, that our entrenched patterns of thinking and behavior are the enemies of creativity and growth. And the longer you allow those patterns to remain unchallenged, the harder they become to divert.

In some cases, this is actually a desirable state. If you're a brain surgeon then we can think of those rivers as expertise that grow deeper with experience. In such a case you probably don't want your surgeon diverting some of those waters into how to brew the perfect cup of coffee. But for someone in a leadership position, in which flexibility is not only desirable but essential, we don't want those rivers to become so entrenched that we can't adapt.

You can do this in trivial areas, such as making choices in your personal life that go against your natural instincts. If you pick up the *Wall Street Journal* every day on the way to work, maybe tomorrow you reach for *Cat Fancy* magazine or *Boating World* magazine. Instead of automatically playing whatever movie is in Netflix's "most watched" spot, you pick a documentary about a subject you know nothing about and would usually ignore.

It sounds a little silly, and I'm not suggesting that this is going to result in some great new learning, but when you make a conscious effort to change your instinctive choices you're teaching yourself to question your decisions and consider trying a different way. You're learning to create new rivulets that might one day become streams and perhaps eventually become whole new rivers.

STATE YOUR INTENTIONS

Performing a gap analysis—comparing actual performance with desired performance—on yourself is a healthy way to review your performance and progress in an area you're looking to work on. All it takes is two questions:

1. Where am I now (with this goal)?
2. Where do I want to be?

Let's do this exercise now with a question around intentionality.

3. How intentional am I with my decision-making in the workplace?
4. How intentional do I want to be with my decision-making in the workplace?

Think about the day's events, the work you've completed, the decisions you've made, and the interactions you had with your team. How many of those activities were performed on autopilot and how many did you think through? In fact, go even further. With how many of those activities did you consciously give yourself room to pause and think through your actions?

Intentionality is such an important ability for everyone, but especially for leaders. The less you exercise intentionality, the more you do things by habit. And the more you do things by habit, the less you think about *why* you're doing them in a certain way or what the impact is. This is problematic because if you develop bad habits, those repeated negative actions will only become more deeply entrenched over time. Even good habits, as great as they are to have, will stagnate if you never take the time to consider them and ask whether there's a better way.

If you have your computer or phone at hand, open up your calendar. If it's anything like mine it'll look like a game of Tetris that has gone badly wrong and you're about to get a "Game Over" screen. That's the nature of being in a role with a lot of responsibilities. Nevertheless, look for some room (or make some room) where you schedule in some time for mindfulness moments. It could be meditation, a short walk, some light exercise, or anything else that gives you space to clear your mind and give your decision-making muscles room to breathe.

It takes practice, but when you have moments in your life where you have room to mentally refresh, you'll find yourself more accustomed to reflecting on what you do in the workplace. This is especially valuable when you can learn to pause before decisions and give yourself a beat before making a call that could have significant repercussions. Once you can do that, you'll often realize, not only that this is a decision too important to make without further consideration, but that it's perfectly fine to delay the decision until you've had time to think it over.

There's nothing wrong (and everything right) with saying, "Actually, I need to think about this some more. I'll come back to you with a decision by the end of the week."

You can then block out some time to review the matter, consider the consequences, and come to an intentional decision.

Learning to be intentional in all different areas of your work is an incredible gift you can give to yourself. You'll make better choices, of course, but you'll also find it easier to live with the outcomes when you know you've made the best decision you could.

START BEING MORE INTENTIONAL

How can you apply this intentionality in the workplace? Start by recognizing that rivers of thinking don't just occur in individuals, they also exist in groups. Your team, especially if they've been working together for some time, will have deep rivers running through their day-to-day activity. Again, in some instances, this is helpful, especially if a river is efficient and gets you from point A to point B without any deviations. But there will almost certainly be some rivers that make unnecessary detours, and no one questions it because those habits run deep.

Sometimes those unhelpful rivers are very obvious. Other times they won't present themselves unless you explore other options. Workshops themed around creativity are excellent for this purpose because they encourage the participants to consider new ideas and new ways of doing things in a safe space where there are no consequences for inventing something that doesn't work. When you engage in creative exercises and then use those occasions to review methods of working, you almost always uncover some surprises.

When I host creativity workshops I like to select a venue that is as far from the world of technology as possible, such as a zoo or an aquarium. Our computers and smartphones are designed to help us accomplish things quickly with as little thought and effort as possible, and that's totally counter to encouraging people to come up with original thoughts. A venue that drags attention away from our devices is a simple counter to that reflex.

Some years ago I attended a workshop in Vermont, and I had

a long drive into what felt like the middle of nowhere. The event wasn't in any of the main cities, such as Burlington or Essex. It was in a tiny place called Goshen with a population of fewer than two hundred people. I wasn't in the best of moods because I was traveling all the way from California, and my sister was about to have her fourth child and I really wanted to be present for that. But I'd made a commitment and I was following through.

After driving for hours I pulled into a national forest with no cell service, and that was followed by even more driving. Eventually I arrived at the Blueberry Hill Inn and I was greeted inside by twenty other people who were there for the workshop. We'd basically taken over the entire inn amongst beautiful surroundings with the goal of learning how to apply creativity to our work habits. It turned out to be the perfect location because, when you're in the middle of nature, technology has a tendency to fade into the background. Everything was old school: flip charts and white boards, no slides or shared docs, or any of the things we were accustomed to using for training events.

And it was kind of perfect. The very first principle we discussed was, you guessed it, Edward DeBona and his rivers of thinking. And what better way to get us into that headspace than to get rid of all the technological crutches that fed those rigid patterns and create room to think differently?

I definitely recommend making your creativity session something that doesn't require technology. But, at the very least, it's a smart move to choose a location that is out of the ordinary for a workshop or in a place that is unfamiliar to everyone. Encouraging new, creative ways of thinking is always best achieved in new environments with new methods of learning.

There are an infinite number of creative exercises you can use in your workshop. A quick Google search will provide you with more ideas than you could try in ten lifetimes. But the one I've found to be most effective is to go right on the nose and try to break your existing workplace rules and methods. Literally, pick one core element of your business or what your team members do and destroy it.

Let's say your business is a pub and you want to explore ways to make your venue more interesting to attract more customers. Take some of the most basic elements of your business and ask, "What would happen if we got rid of that?"

The goal is to take a concept to the extreme, to its natural conclusion, and then dial it down into something achievable and see what that would look like. It's a method of encouraging expansive thinking that goes beyond the normal thought processes you use every day, which usually take place within tight boundaries. The imagination is allowed to expand to its limit, right into the realms of fantasy, and is then eased back down into the real world.

It's like doing weight training but for creative thinking. You lift the heaviest object you can, and then gently lower it. You repeat this often enough and subsequently create strength and flexibility.

You can apply this exercise to any element of your business. Your team, for instance, likely has a set of rules, policies, and habits they employ with little or no thought. Pick one of those rules and invite your team to imagine breaking it, taking it to its limit, and then discuss what the consequences could be. The end result might just be that this rule is fine and nothing needs to change. Other times, you might spot opportunities to try doing something differently. Either way, you're giving everyone space to get out of their rut, their rivers of thinking, and interrogate what they do in the workspace and why.

At their heart, I believe most people value the opportunity to be creative. Even the most logically-minded, pattern-preferring engineer will likely appreciate the opportunity to exercise their ingenuity and come up with new ideas. So, no matter what kinds of work you do, there are real benefits to encouraging creativity among your team.

I've seen organizations label one of their departments as the "creative team." As lovely as this is for those involved, this can be the kiss of death to everyone else. You're basically telling them, none too subtly, that they're not required to be, or capable of being, creative. What a sad message to send. Every team can benefit from even just a sprinkling of creativity, especially if it stops their rivers of thinking from driving too deep. But it won't happen automatically. You need to encourage it through your feedback, example, and through specifically engineered team-building events that have creativity at their core.

I recently attended a lecture from Bozoma Saint John, the former CMO of Netflix. She published a memoir in 2023 about the challenges of losing her husband to cancer and, as a result, being a single parent.* Her story is extraordinary but the message I most connected with was the idea that people too often wait for a major tragedy, such as a severe illness or a death, before they take time to review their life and think about whether there are things they would like to change.

In a small way, this can also apply to your team members. They may be operating on autopilot at work, and only stop to take stock

* *The Urgent Life: My Story of Love, Loss, and Survival*

of where their career is going and whether they're really satisfied with their lot when something significant changes, such as a bad performance review or bout of poor mental health. Far better to help your team, on a regular basis, find the space to review what they're doing and see if there are positive changes they can make that will improve their results and their job satisfaction.

And don't ignore yourself in this process.

PROACTIVE LEADERSHIP

My hope is that these chapters, the stories within, and the recommended exercises and team events will help you to be intentional and thoughtful in how you develop and exercise your leadership. Don't wait until your unhappiness in your position makes you contemplate quitting, or a new manager that you struggle to get along with makes your position untenable before you make time to proactively consider your role and whether or not you're being true to your authentic self. Get ahead of things now.

This isn't a rallying call to always move onward and upward. It's a recommendation that you make your career decisions and your work habits intentionally and be sure that you're really heading in the direction that is right for you and those around you.

I see a lot of people who are laser-focused on an upward trajectory and are always setting targets for when their next promotion is going to happen. There's an admirable aspect to this drive—providing they take the time to enjoy each stage; otherwise burnout is a very real possibility—but this isn't the only way.

It might seem like escaping rivers of thinking means always

striving to raise the bar for what you're achieving, but actually, the reverse can also be true. If you've only ever had the mindset that success is measured by how high you can climb the ladder, this too can be a river of thinking that may or may not serve you.

This is such an important question to ask because career advancement on its own won't bring you happiness and satisfaction. It needs to be coupled with a clear idea of why you're pursuing it and to what end. Are you pursuing that next promotion because it's a clear, intentional choice you're making, or is it because society is telling you that you "have" to be a manager, or you "have" to earn more, or you "have" to upgrade to a larger house? Are you dissatisfied with your current position because you know you're capable of so much more and you're determined to reach your true potential, or are you very happy and grateful to be in the position you're in and your true preference is to continue excelling in what you're already doing?

One of my favorite books, *Immunity to Change**, has an exercise in which you ask the "why" question ten different times to allow you get to the heart of your true motivations.

I've made a New Year's resolution to go to the gym every day.

Great, but why?

Because I want to be healthier?

Why?

Because I'm getting older and I want to live many more years yet.

Why?

* *Immunity to Change: How to Overcome It and Unlock the Potential in Yourself and Your Organization* (Leadership for the Common Good)

Because I'm afraid of death?

Why?

Because I'm afraid I'll leave important things unfinished or important words unspoken?

Why?

Because I don't have a good relationship with my daughter and there are things we haven't fixed?

Why?

Because I'm too busy at work and with the rest of my family?

Why?

Because it's easier to focus on the things that are in the here and now than do the hard things?

Why?

Because doing the hard thing is going to hurt?

Why?

Because I don't think an open and frank conversation with my daughter is going to go well.

Why?

I don't know…

It's normal to get to a point in this mental exchange where you don't know the answer. And that's a good thing. Because now you know where the sticking point is. In the above example, if this person figures out why they think reconciling with their daughter is going to go badly, then they may be able to do something about it to change the expected result.

This is perhaps an extreme example, but it's not uncommon for simple decisions, when interrogated, to reveal a more profound truth. Going to the gym every day was never going to stick as a resolution because the real underlying desire was to fix a family problem. That's the real resolution that needed to be made.

You can do this exercise with any situation, and you can either do it alone, or with a trusted friend or family member to guide you. And it's especially valuable when making decisions around how you exercise your leadership and how you plot the course of your career.

It's only when you pin down your motivations that your rivers of thinking expose themselves. After that, it's up to you what you decide to do about it.

REFLECTION QUESTIONS: PATTERNS OF LEARNING

- How enthusiastic are you about learning new things?
- What steps can you take to strengthen your interest in developing new skills and knowledge?
- Would you benefit from working with a coach?
- Which of your rivers of thinking are potentially hindering your growth?
- Which of your rivers of thinking are helpful?
- How can you tackle your potentially harmful rivers of thinking?
- How can you add more windows in your schedule for mindful reflection?

CHAPTER 9

PATTERNS OF LEADERSHIP

* * *

WHAT DOES YOUR CANVAS LOOK LIKE?

A few years ago my father celebrated his eightieth birthday and we got him a sweatshirt with a shamrock logo—a symbol that, for many decades, has been his trademark. He literally carries around a packet of shamrock stickers and plants one every place he goes. If he pays you a visit, chances are good you'll find a new sticker left on your computer or a lamp.

But there's a deeper meaning to it.

His catchphrase is "Do great things," and he says it often to encourage and motivate those around him. When he's with the grandkids you'll hear him say, "Hey, James, are you off to do great things today?" Those shamrocks are not just a reminder of his presence, but a reminder of his desire for all of his children and grandchildren to strive for meaning.

Do you have a catchphrase? You probably do whether you realize it or not. When you eventually pass (hopefully many decades from now), your loved ones will likely gather around and reminisce about some of the things you most frequently said. It could be an unusual greeting. Or something you often said when leaving the house. Or something you always said when sharing a meal with your family. Those are the kinds of things that people love about their close friends and family and are often the most treasured memories.

Don't worry if you don't have anything like that, or if you can't think of one. We don't always notice these mannerisms in ourselves. But I want you to think about it because the things you're most known for saying, your pattern of words, are often an insight into what you're putting into the world.

We talked about this intentionality earlier. Remember Chris in chapter 4 who was always "busy" and "tired?" This was the message she was putting out into the world until she became aware of it and changed. Regardless of whether or not you already have frequently-used language that you're known for, you have an opportunity to make a conscious effort to find something positive and encouraging and have that be your mantra.

And whatever you settle on, this is going to go at the top of your leadership canvas.

This isn't a literal canvas—which is good news for me because I can barely draw a convincing stick figure—but it's good to think of it as such. Your leadership canvas is a metaphor that exists in your mind and encompasses all the elements of who you are as a leader, the journey that brought you here, and the road that you're consciously planning to travel.

This, to my mind, is so much more powerful than viewing your career as a ladder you're climbing. Because in that word picture, every rung climbed leaves you putting your boots on what came before and literally leaving it behind. Whereas a leadership canvas is a mosaic of everything so you can drink in the whole thing in a single mental image. It consists of your values, triumphs, mistakes, disappointments, joys, stories, and the people who impacted you most along the way.

And your canvas is never fully complete. There will always be room to add a little more here and there. The image will keep expanding to fit the size and shape of your leadership journey and will always become richer and more intricate over time.

What does your leadership canvas look like so far? Is it full of powerful images or is it quite sparsely populated so far? Is it mainly positivity and light, or is there some negativity and darkness that is in urgent need of being surrounded by something more hopeful?

In this final exercise we're going to add some broad brush strokes to your canvas by reviewing the subjects we've covered. Not in the form of a summary, but in the form of a series of related questions. What I'd like you to do is consider these questions carefully, and write out your answers (physically, in a notebook, if possible). The most critical answers you uncover are going to find their way onto your leadership canvas and help you turn your masterpiece into something you can proudly hang in your mind palace. Here's a summary of chapter reflection questions to form your canvas:

PATTERNS OF SELF

What kind of leader do you want to be?

What kind of leader would your team describe you as being?

What kind of leader might you have been falsely assuming you *should* be?

How do you feel about the idea of someone referring to you as a leader?

Is your work personality the same as your "at home" personality and, if not, why not?

PATTERNS OF FEEDBACK

How do you believe you respond to criticism?

How did you respond to the last meaningful criticism you received?

How well do you know your team members' personalities beyond their work abilities?

Have you completed (or are you planning to complete) a feedback assessment?

Has your team completed (or are you planning to complete) a feedback assessment?

Are you familiar with your weaknesses and how you can turn them into strengths?

Are you familiar with your strengths and how they could potentially become weaknesses?

What have you done (or are planning to do) to assist and empower any members of your team who are, in some manner, a minority?

When was the last time, if ever, that you blamed the lettuce?

PATTERNS OF VALUES

What are some of your positive traits that you would like your team to imitate?

What are some of your less desirable traits that you wouldn't like your team to imitate?

How would you describe the culture of your team?

What would you like the culture of your team to be?

What can you start doing (or stop doing) that might influence the culture of your team in the direction you'd like it to be?

What contradictions are there between how you'd like your team culture to be, and how you act as a leader?

How well do your instructions to your team reach the individual members?

What changes could you make to your communication methods that will make it easier for your team members to stay abreast of your instructions?

What does being a trim tab for your organization mean to you?

What event could you create to help you learn more about your team's values?

How much flexibility do your team members have to approach work in a manner that fits their individual modes of working?

What biases might you hold that could negatively affect your abilities as a leader?

PATTERNS OF STORIES

What message or attitude are you putting into the world when you interact with work colleagues?

What story can you tell that reflects your most cherished value(s)?

Which stories from other leaders (either from this book or from your personal experience) most resonate with you and why?

PATTERNS OF HIGH-PERFORMING TEAMS

How would you rate your team in the following five areas (mark them on a scale of 0-5)?

- **Psychological safety:** Can we take risks on this team without feeling insecure or embarrassed?
- **Dependability:** Can we count on each other to do high quality work on time?
- **Structure & clarity:** Are goals, roles, and execution plans on our team clear?
- **Meaning of work:** Are we working on something that is personally important for each of us?
- **Impact of work:** Do we fundamentally believe that the work we're doing matters?

How would your team members rate your team in the above five areas?

How comfortable are you in giving negative feedback to a

team member?

Have you ever avoided giving feedback to a team member because you were anxious about how it might play out?

Does your company or department mission/vision/value statement reflect the reality of your team's work experience?

PATTERNS OF RESILIENCE

What does your kintsugi vessel look like?

Which members of your team could use your help repairing their cracks with gold?

What steps are you taking to build resilience?

When can you arrange your next "off-site" meeting?

How could you improve how you deal with conflict with your team members?

PATTERNS OF CONNECTION

Do you have any habits relating to prioritizing technology over those who are present?

How would you rate your ability to truly listen when people speak?

How would your team members rate your ability to truly listen when people speak?

What conscious efforts can you make to forge better connections with people in the workplace?

What opportunities do you have to practice and develop your connecting skills?

PATTERNS OF LEARNING

How enthusiastic are you about learning new things?

What steps can you take to develop your interest in developing new skills and knowledge?

Would you benefit from working with a coach?

Which of your rivers of thinking are potentially hindering your growth?

Which of your rivers of thinking are helpful?

How can you tackle your potentially harmful rivers of thinking?

How can you add more windows in your schedule for mindful reflection?

YOUR LEADERSHIP PHILOSOPHY

When our family engages in our dinnertime ritual of going around the table and identifying something that we're grateful for, occasionally someone will struggle because, frankly, they've had a crappy day. It happens to all of us from time to time, and when it does it can be very difficult to find something meaningful to contribute. Present pain can blind us to the joys and blessings that still exist. When that happens, that person is given a free pass—not to say nothing, but to simply affirm that they're grateful to be sitting at a table with food on their plate, surrounded by people who love them.

In truth, even then, that person might not be feeling the gratitude in the moment. But it keeps the routine going, and strengthens that gratitude muscle that helps us to avoid falling into negative patterns of thinking.

We can take the same approach with our leadership canvas and the personalized model that we're putting together. Your method is unique to you and, as you apply the brush strokes of your leadership philosophy to your canvas, you can learn to connect your strengths and abilities with your values and priorities.

This must be a very deliberate act. The answers to the questions in the previous section that you're writing down and the other observations that you make about yourself are creating a unique image that will help you visualize the kind of leader you were always destined to become.

And there *will* be times when the picture becomes hazy. When you've had an uncomfortable conflict or you've made some bad decisions or received some negative feedback, it can be difficult to maintain confidence in your methods. But in the same way that even a bad day can contain reasons for gratitude, so, too, shortcomings in your leadership abilities can reveal hidden strengths and resilience.

In those moments, recall those occasions in your career—and even earlier—when you demonstrated elements of your leadership abilities or witnessed the positive effects of your actions.

- Someone specifically asked to be on my team because they wanted to work with me.
- A project I helmed was a rousing success and helped a number of other participants move up in their career.
- I mentored a junior executive who is now in a senior leadership position at a Fortune 500 company.
- I led my college basketball team to a state championship final.

- I was one of the founding members of an amateur orchestra and I was instrumental in keeping the group together, playing every Friday night, for five years.

You will find it helpful to write these down so you can easily refer back to them whenever you need, but especially on occasions when you find your confidence wavering and you're finding it hard to keep the faith.

These memories are fixed points in your life that are the key images in your leadership canvas. They'll help you through tough moments. But, even more importantly, they will spur you on to be the leader you need to be.

And don't wait.

You can be a leader wherever you are, in any job position, with any personality type, and with any management style. But it won't happen unless you make it happen. Have confidence in yourself, in who you are, and in the unique combination of abilities and values that you bring to the table. It's your individuality that makes your voice valuable and worth sharing.

Sometimes people are afraid to speak because they think that if what they had to say was worthwhile, someone else would already have said it. This is flatly untrue. It's impossible for someone else to speak up and express something that comes out of our own unique point of view. So, when you censor yourself, you're not only placing unreasonable limits on yourself, you're also robbing everybody around you of your valuable contribution.

Your true value is in who you are. The real you. The authentic you. The voice that is yours and yours alone.

Once you understand that, you can go do great things.

EPILOGUE

* * *

LEADERSHIP FOR EVERYONE

Google is for everyone. That's one of its core values and if you look through any of the key sites such as Google Careers, the Google Blog, and Google Support, you'll find this phrasing used liberally. Careers for everyone. Code for everyone. Design for everyone. And the most important version: Build for everyone. You can, if you wish, even buy an official Google t-shirt with this message emblazoned on it.

So, what about "leadership for everyone"? What would that look like? I already said in the previous chapter that I believe everyone has the opportunity and the ability to lead if they apply themselves to it. But how would that work in practice?

WHAT IS A LEADER?

It's interesting to note that if you ask someone—adult or child—to draw a picture of a leader, they'll typically draw a king, or someone leading a march, or shouting into a megaphone, or standing on a hill with their sword drawn. But most people don't draw a picture of themselves.

Maybe everyone is just too modest to think of themselves as an archetypal leader, but it's more likely that we have an inflated idea of what a leader is and what they look like. Our mind automatically goes to the great heroes and presidents and business legends of days gone by, when in reality a leader is simply someone who leads others in some way.

Even in an everyday setting, such as an office space, we still typically think of a leader as a charismatic person who speaks loudly and is blessed with great vision and insight. And yet when we think about it more carefully we quickly realize that this is only one type of leader.

Leaders, in the real world, come in all shapes and sizes. The quietest, smallest, least charismatic person in a group may still automatically be looked to as a leader because there's a sense that they have a certain level of intelligence and composure that makes them best suited to the role.

We can take this to extremes. You could have a team made up of nine experienced businessmen, all over the age of 60, and one 21-year-old, female intern. The young woman of the group is the last person you would expect to be the leader, but if the team has taken on a project to create a music event for high school students, and a key requirement is to choose music acts that will appeal to this audience, who do you think they're going to lean on to lead that project?

The reality is that, to a greater or lesser degree, we're all called upon at various times to lead in some capacity. Your success in that role will often be a result of your level of confidence and training, but experience also counts for a lot. And you can't obtain leadership experience without acting in that role.

Even then, if you set out to develop your skills as a leader, you don't read a book or attend a workshop and then instantly morph into a leader, like Popeye after guzzling a can of spinach. It takes time and effort to go from being a leader in name to being a leader in practice. Can a team lead be said to be a leader if people don't understand what they're thinking, can't share their vision, and aren't willing to follow them? There are many styles of leadership, but those qualities are the bare minimum for success.

The reason I want you to think of leadership in these terms is because I said, right from the outset, that this book isn't going to tell you *how* to be a leader. If there's any quality or value that I'd love to see all leaders, of every stripe, embrace, it would be to take the view that everyone can benefit from striving to develop and display leadership qualities.

A strong leader is not a dictator who rules with an iron fist. A strong leader is one who is confident enough to share power and responsibility with others. If you can view your team not as a group of subordinates, but as a group of potential leaders, then this empowers them to mature in their career and gives you a stronger pool of resources that can support you and your organization in your work.

For example, if someone on your team falls out with another team member and they come to you to resolve it, that should send shivers down your spine. Going to Mummy or Daddy to fix a fight is something that you do as a child and is something you eventually (hopefully) grow out of. The ideal would be for those two team members to have the confidence and resilience to be able to sit down and settle the matter between themselves. That should be their first port of call. You should be the last.

If you view your team as leaders in development you will naturally be inclined to set up your team in a way that empowers them with responsibility and a level of autonomy. You should be looking to influence your team in a positive way, to connect people, and to be a champion and ally for everyone. But this is far better achieved by setting the tone and leading by example than by trying to micromanage every detail of your team's day.

You don't have time for that. You're busy. You have a lot of responsibility. If you add to that, trying to run your team like it's a daycare, then you're in for a world of exhaustion and frustration.

WORKING TOGETHER

One analogy in leadership workshops is the migrating geese, flying in an efficient "V" formation. The goose at the front expends the most energy, with the rest of the flock benefiting from less wind and air resistance, as well as lift created by air rolling off the wingtips of the leader. At regular intervals, one of the trailing geese will switch places with the leader so it can rest. It's a lovely metaphor but it's also a bit of a strange one to use for leadership qualities because geese don't actually have an overall leader. They act more as a democracy, taking turns to lead the charge.

I find it more helpful to think of the geese as your team, and you as an overseer, encouraging the geese so stay in formation and support each other to keep going. Your team members shouldn't be reliant on one individual to do all the work and should work together to get to their destination.

And there's another, lesser known, element of the geese migration phenomenon. If one of the geese becomes sick or so exhausted that it has to land, two other geese will break formation and join the goose until it's recovered. After that, they'll re-join the flock as soon as they're able.*

This is such a beautiful analogy for how a team can support and care for each other. Isn't this how you'd like your team to be? Taking turns to lead the flight and taking responsibility for struggling members are all amazing leadership qualities. This is what I mean by leadership for everyone. Imagine leading your team in such an inclusive way that you empower them to support and care for each other, to the point where you're only needed for major or unexpected incidents.

Any leadership style can achieve this epitome of leadership principles because it is independent of your specific management approach. Your leadership canvas is unique and your team's individual leadership canvases, even those that are new and barely touched by color, will also be distinctive. Whatever kind of leader you're aiming to be, I urge you to extend that same opportunity to those around you.

If you embrace the exercises and thoughtful questions described in this book, you'll gather huge quantities of information about yourself, all of which are invaluable to your growth as a leader and in your career aspirations. So, take that knowledge and help others to achieve the same.

In the introduction to this book I said it has been a privilege to

* https://birdsandwetlands.com/how-do-geese-decide-who-leads

help others grow and shine in their career. It's a joy that is quite unlike anything else.

I want you to share that experience as well. The greatest leaders, in my view, are the ones who inspire and shape other leaders in their wake. What higher ambition could there be than to leave the world in a better place than which you found it?

Be bold, enthusiastic, and ambitious in your leadership journey. But always remember that journeys are best experienced in the company of others.

Bring others along with you for the ride.

Keep growing and shine your brilliance into the world.

PATTERNS OF GRATITUDE

* * *

(ACKNOWLEDGMENTS)

I am so grateful to my amazing community of friends and family for their love and support throughout the journey of writing this book. I couldn't have done it without you! Here are extra special shout-outs to folks who've gone above and beyond . . .

Grateful for my loving husband, Jim, who encourages all my wild ideas and helps me follow my dreams. Thanks for being the family rock throughout the writing and editing process.

Grateful for my brilliant kids, James and Lily. You inspire me every day. I'm so proud to be your mom!

Grateful for my incredible parents. My mom, the world's best English teacher, for both the "red pen" mark-ups on my grammar as well as the "gold stars" on my revisions. My dad, for being the ultimate role model for leadership and a life well lived. Thank you both for teaching me the gifts of empathy, gratitude, and a strong work ethic.

Grateful for my big extended family—Egans, LeSueurs,

Hegmanns, Smiths, Martins, Loughrans, Gruendels, Kenworthys, and McKennas, especially my cousins, Clare Gruendel and Kate Kenworthy, for always cheering me on.

Grateful for my amazing team for their encouragement to write down and share this impactful work: Shana Hawley, Kate Fleming, Whitney Cox, Jay Friedman, Sabrina Vande Cotte, Hannah Kopeikin, Hannah Louis, Tyler Tory-Murphy, Mecca Williams, Karina Opper, Michael Munoz, and Claire Griffin.

Extra grateful for my workshop teammates and partners: Jenni Shideler and Weiqi Kuang, who make each session we run together special with their attention to detail, high bar for excellence, and magic dust that makes everything sparkle.

Grateful for the ultimate strategic thinking partners: Leo and Niki Marin, founders of the Leadership Supply Co. Leo is one of the driving forces behind me writing this book in the first place. Thank you for countless inspiring conversations, true partnership, and for making the world a better place.

Grateful for the incredible, smart, visionary leaders I've had the pleasure to work for and learn from, especially Lorraine Twohill, Sarah Armstrong, and Suzanne Dalcourt.

Grateful for all the alumni from my leadership programs and coaching sessions over the years. Thank you for your stories and inspiration! Especially those I included in the book: Amelia Eddleman, Nicole Huynh, Mansha Tandon, Max Joseph, and Eduardo Samuel.

Grateful for all my brilliant colleagues and mentors over the years: Danielle Tiedt, Lisa Gevelber, Marie Gulin-Merle, Simon Kahn, Jeff Whipps, Yonca Dervisoglu, Eileen Mannion, Alison Wagonfeld, Andy Berndt, Robert Wong, Ben Malbon, Kate

Stanford, Beth Ames, Dede Orraca-Tetteh, Andrew Schulte, Daniel Kim, Ramin Baghai, Amy Brennan, Cenk Bulbul, Jesse Haines, Bethany Poole, Enshalla Anderson, Sadie Toma, Penny Chu, Sapna Chadha, Maya Shankar, Suzie Reider, Lexi Reese, Debbie Newhouse, Khee Lee, Scott Falzone, Courtney Rose, Brian Glaser, Jim Lecinski, Naina Jacobson-Esposito, Laura Eriksen, Brian Deluca, Pete Simmons, Michele Aptman, Kirk Vallis, Kathrin O'Sullivan, Amanda Foster, Ann Pellegrini, Terrence Maltbia, Eric Bradlow, Kathy Pearson, Kevin Carroll, and Eric Boggs.

Grateful for my favorite professor at Boston College, Paul Reynolds, for inspiring a love of books and boundless creativity.

Grateful for my college roommates, Julie Rollauer, Molly Donovan, Danielle Acerra, and MaryBeth Heyd, for making life more fun and being wonderful listeners.

Grateful for lifelong, supportive friends: Bill and Dana Lehnert, Katie and Kieran Hanrahan, Carissa and Lance Arneson, Matt and Melanie Lambert, JT and Andrea Deignan, Joe and Jessica Brantuk, BethAnn and Joe Arlia, Scott and Michelle Clark, Diane and Tom McClelland, Joyce and Barry Lord, William and Diane Venezia, Paula and Brendan McGovern, Colleen and Pete Denoto, Christine and Vydas Marijosius, Julie Weyne, and Gavin Scotti.

Grateful for my Vermont mountain friends—sharing stories around the firepit with you all makes winter not only bearable but downright wonderful! Especially the Lehnerts, Schultzes, Weynes, Lockwoods, and Walkers.

Grateful for Mark and Jayne Battey, owners and founders of Miramar Farms in San Mateo County, California for their beautiful space to gather, learn and grow.

Grateful for my dogs who make me smile every day—shout out to the dog park crew!

ABOUT THE AUTHOR

Suzanne Martin has over twenty-five years of experience in learning and development and sales and marketing, the past sixteen at Google taking on many different roles including most recently as the Director of Global Marketer Training. She has facilitated hundreds of leadership and team development workshops inside and outside of Google.

Martin is an accredited coach with the International Coaching Federation, has earned a coaching certificate from Columbia University, and has been a part of the Forbes Inc. Coaches Council since 2017. She is accredited in Brain-Based Coaching through the Neuroleadership Institute, Multipliers, Myers-Briggs Type Indicator, Insights Discovery, Hogan Assessments, ATD Instructional Design, and the Leadership Circle. Her team won a Brandon Hall award for leadership development as a best certification program in 2022. She is currently a member of Chief, the executive women's network.

Martin graduated cum laude from Boston College and has a project management certificate from Stanford. She lives in New York with her husband, two children, and two Australian Shepherds, Coco and Waffles. She's an avid skier, adventurous traveler, and lifelong learner.

in /suzannemartinleadership